A Celebration

A Celebration

« THE OFFICIAL STORY OF FORTY YEARS IN SHOW BUSINESS »

ANDRE
DEUTSCH

First published in Great Britain in 1998

This edition first published in 1999
by André Deutsch Ltd
76 Dean Street, London W1V 5HA
www.vci.co.uk

A catalogue record for this title is available from the British Library

ISBN 0 233 99455-6

Designed by Robert Kelland and Peta Waddington

Printed and bound in Great Britain
by Butler & Tanner, Frome and London

Contents

A Celebration

Foreword

In the early years rock 'n' roll was what it was all about. After the release of my first single in 1958 things started to happen very quickly and in what seems no time at all, here I am celebrating my forty years in the music industry.

Decade by decade, *A Celebration* is just that - a celebration of those forty years. Kate Shaw has helped me compile the story of my career. She has looked through numerous archives, performed many hours of research and she has drawn on what I remember from my forty years in this exciting industry. She has helped put those memories into words. Forty years is a long time and unfortunately memories fade. I believe what follows is a fair representation of four decades of making music, and I am sorry if I get anything wrong.

When I look back at television clips of me singing *Move It* I can remember the thrill of that early success. Forty years later I still know that thrill. I have had the amazing privilege of experiencing forty rewarding years of working at what I love.

Thank you.

Cliff

The Early Years

★

_____

My life changed for
ever in 1958. Sudden and
unexpected fame carried me along
at a breathless pace. And that
excitement has never left me,
as each year brings its surprises
and continued success beyond
the wildest dreams of
Harry Webb, the office clerk
from Cheshunt.

Cliff

An early stage appearance as Ratty in the Cheshunt Secondary Modern School Dramatic Society production of Toad of Toad Hall.

At the beginning of 1958 I was 17, not long out of school with one O-level, and earning £4.15s a week. On a good day I would rush off from my job as a filing clerk and sing rock 'n' roll in a pub or youth club in the evening. Twelve months later, at 18, I was a celebrity pop star with a number one hit, a major tour under my belt, a regular spot in a top television show and I was about to make a film. I couldn't walk in the street without attracting screaming girls. Suddenly my whole life came under public scrutiny, but I had absolutely no complaints – this was the only career I'd ever wanted. The days whirled by in a series of fantastic opportunities and I had no idea what was going to happen next.

For all I knew then, my career might be over by the time I was twenty. I never even considered that from this mind-blowing year of success would grow the forty years in the music business that I am able to celebrate with this book. It seems incredible that so much happened so quickly, but when I look back I don't look for rhyme or reason, I see a happy, lucky young man – and I'm glad it was me!

The life-changing hit was *Move It*, recorded at my first session at EMI and written by Ian Samwell on the top of a Greenline number 715 bus on the way to Norrie Paramor's office for an audition. A jittery Cliff and the Drifters lugged their amplifier up to recording studio 2 at EMI in Abbey Road, where we were to make our first record, produced by Norrie Paramor, but we relaxed when we started playing. I remember Ian Samwell sprawled out on the studio floor, making some last minute changes to the lyrics and Ernie Shear creating the now legendary intro to *Move It*. Our first Columbia recording session took place on July 24. It was customary to use session men – in this case Ernie Shear on guitar and Frank Clarke on bass. It was great for me that *Move It* became the A-side of our first single, because it meant that I started my career with an original song penned by new writers – in those days it was unheard of for a British group to record a song written by one of its members.

Move It never fails to bring back great memories for me. I can remember singing it in the far corner of Studio 2, and having my first publicity photos for Columbia Records taken in the same spot. And when I picture the studio, Norrie Paramor is always there too. He became something of a father figure to me over the years. I have always been grateful for his unfailing encouragement and enthusiasm. Norrie had been in the music business since he was fifteen, as a band leader, a pianist and, for the previous nine years, a music director. He took home an early recording of *Schoolboy Crush* to try out on his teenage daughter Caroline and told us, 'She flipped when she heard it! But she preferred the B-side, *Move It*.'

The very first track I put on tape for EMI was *Schoolboy Crush*, a song that had been recorded in the States by Bobby Helms and had made the charts a few months before. At that time it was usually the producer who selected the songs to be recorded, so I was happy to be allowed to record *Move It* as the B-side. However, our song – penned on the bus trip – proved to be the most popular side of the single. In fact it has come to be regarded as a landmark in British music – *Move It* is now generally considered to be the very first all-British rock record.

I sing once through the song on the original recording, then there's an instrumental section and I go through it again. Ian had only got as far as the first verse and chorus before we had to get off the bus, and it took another thirty odd years to get the second verse – Ian sent Hank Marvin a new lyric when Hank re-recorded the song in 1984 with me as guest vocalist.

Luckily for me, Jack Good was one of the few people who had bothered to listen to the B-side of *Schoolboy Crush*. Jack had previously introduced rock 'n' roll into a BBC TV programme called *6.5 Special* and he was launching a new show, *Oh Boy!* for the rival channel ABC Television. The point of *Move It*'s lyrics – that rock 'n' roll was not a passing phase but here to stay and gaining strength – appealed to Jack. He insisted that I sing *Move It*, and not *Schoolboy Crush*, to help set the new British rock 'n' roll tone for the first show of his *Oh Boy!* series, which was transmitted live from the Empire Theatre in Hackney.

EMI wasted no time in rewording the adverts for my record and *Move It* became the A-side. I was a little apprehensive about auditioning for Jack Good, but at least it couldn't go much worse than our first stab at TV. A week earlier the BBC *6.5 Special* crew had signalled us to stop playing mid-song and shown us the door, with the encouraging words, 'Sorry, lads, but your style's not suitable. It's not likely to last, either.'

After watching me sing *Don't Bug Me Baby* and *Move It* at rehearsals, Jack seemed pleased. 'I was relieved when you turned up for audition looking like a normal human being,' Jack told me. 'Usually when I hear a wonderful record I think, "oh yeah, he's probably got three chins or four eyes, something has to make that great sound wrong for television" – I couldn't believe that you would look any good.'

It was an easy step from Harry Webb to Cliff Richard. The more I saw my name in big letters the more I liked it.

I took this as a compliment. Nevertheless, he wanted me to make some changes: 'Your style has too much in common with Elvis. Get rid of the sideburns. Don't play the guitar, just stand there. Lower your head, keep your arms still at your sides, and look up through your eyebrows at the camera.'

The image was mean and moody and smiling wasn't allowed, but I carried on curling my lip whenever I thought of it. Jack explained how it would work for television. He was the one who got me to consider the visual details of my performance. Look at any young singer who is serious about the way they look and they still follow the same pattern, the 'smouldering' bit never fails. But in 1958 to smoulder to any degree was very bold.

With my first proper pay cheque from Columbia Records, for the grand sum of £60, I'd bought a television set for my family, and within a few weeks they were watching me on it.

The *New Musical Express* described my performance thus: 'The most crude exhibitionism ever seen on TV. If we are expected to believe that Cliff Richard was acting naturally then consideration for medical treatment before it's too late may be advisable.'

A centre spread in the *Daily Mirror* was headlined 'Is the boy too sexy for television?'

The outfit I wore for *Oh Boy!* became a trademark used in every Cliff Richard impersonation for years: a long pink teddy-boy jacket, black shirt, pink tie, grey suede shoes and luminous pink socks. At the beginning of the series Marty Wilde got all the attention and the screams. Then *Move It* moved into the charts and everything changed. For the first show, zilch in terms of live audience response; for my second show, I couldn't hear myself singing for the screams and my jacket was nearly torn off as I tried to leave the theatre. And that's how my story started.

My ambition to be a singer had been well and truly fired in one memorable moment when I was 14. On a Saturday afternoon in May 1956, as I was walking along Waltham Cross with a group of friends, I heard a few lines of *Heartbreak Hotel* on the radio of a parked car. It gave me goosebumps. The moment I heard Elvis my ambitions became clear. I knew then with absolute certainty that I wanted to sing and be part of this new world of rock 'n' roll. Before we could find out who the singer was the driver came out of a shop and drove off, but we'd heard enough to be hooked.

My friends and I all went off home and tuned in to Radio Luxembourg and the American Forces Network until one of us found out who was making such a fantastic sound. From then on I chased that dream. Elvis's music became part of my life, and with it came Bill Haley, Little Richard, Jerry Lee Lewis, Buddy Holly, The Everly Brothers, Chuck Berry – all the greats, and the best-ever exponents of rock 'n' roll because the sound then was basic and full of beat.

The rawness was to change when The Beatles came along and cleaned up rock 'n' roll. Even though their music still represented all sorts of things a mother wouldn't want her children to be associated with, The Beatles nevertheless got rock 'n' roll played in front of the Queen. When I started rocking the music was a much more raw and shockingly dangerous vehicle.

My sister Donna and I would save all our pocket money until we could buy an Elvis album and take it out of the bag as soon as we got out of the shop so that everyone could see we were Elvis fans. Each evening as soon as we got home from school the album would go on the record player, with the volume turned up as loud as possible, and stay on until late at night or until someone complained.

Like millions of other teenagers I'd listen to Elvis while standing in front of the mirror practising the hip swivel and the curling lip, pausing only to comb my hair into a more bouffant quiff. At 14 nothing else mattered, the record player was my life!

My first 'pop' performance was at the Holy Trinity Youth Club Dance, then I found the confidence to form a group called the Quintones with friends from school – Beryl Molineux, Freda Johnson, John Vince and Frances Slade. We sang unaccompanied and did a

My dad bought my first guitar for my sixteenth birthday for the princely sum of £27. He taught me the three-chord trick and I never looked back. Most of my peers had to choose between the services and the local factory – luckily I escaped into music.

lot of harmonies, after which I got to do my own 'spot' of Elvis numbers – *Heartbreak Hotel, Don't Be Cruel* – still unaccompanied and, if not very impressive, probably quite a spectacle.

When I was 16 my Dad bought me a guitar, no doubt realising by this time that my obsession with music wasn't going to go away. That first guitar cost £27, which represented quite a long-term financial commitment for my father because he couldn't afford to pay cash. Having played banjo in a trad jazz band when he was younger, Dad was able to teach me the useful chord progression of G, C and D7. You can play almost anything with those chords – and I did, all the time trying to make every chord sound like wild rock 'n' roll.

My last year at school had little to do with passing exams but was an important part of my education, in terms of the influence of friends I met there. I was part of a very close and lively group of pupils and our teacher, Jay Norris, has remained a friend.

Making a living from singing was still my dream when I left school but, with one O-level to my name (in English Language), I took a summer job as a tomato picker, after which I had to see the sense in taking an office job my father had found for me.

That's how I began 1958 – a Credit Control Clerk (aka teaboy) at Atlas Lamps on the Great Cambridge Road in Enfield. I cycled eight miles or so to work with my father every morning, we sat at opposite ends of a huge administration office, spoke at tea breaks, and cycled home together at the end of the day.

At Atlas Lamps I did not excel. I found the job so mind-numbingly boring that, although I tried to hide it, my father must have noticed my eyes glazing over or my feet tapping out a rock rhythm. And he must have been sadly disappointed with my performance. Part of my work involved filing accounts by UK region – South West, Midlands, North East and so on – but my knowledge of geography was so poor that the job took me hours. Electric bulbs and their associated accounts failed to grab any of my interest. I only came alive after work, listening to rock 'n' roll or practising on my guitar.

The Quintones had disintegrated by September 1957, and the stage outfit I bought with one of my first wage packets from Atlas Lamps came out for shows with the Dick Teague Skiffle Group and, soon after, the Drifters. It was a black sweater with a length of black wool threaded around the red stripe that ran down one arm. I entered a couple of talent contests and got nowhere, but I was undeterred. A future involving Atlas Lamps was possible but not desirable.

On one memorably lucky morning it was too rainy to cycle to work, so I made a rare bus journey and found myself sitting next to Frances Slade. She remembered my enthusiastic Elvis impersonations and encouraged me to get in touch with her boyfriend, Terry Smart. He was the drummer of the Dick Teague Skiffle Group, which was looking for a singer. Frances said she'd put a word in for me.

I spent that night at home learning to play simple skiffle chord sequences in three different keys and the next night I sought out Terry Smart. My audition with Dick Teague went well. However, after two months of folksy skiffle songs I'd had enough. There was rock

Cliff Richard ✳ 15

I wanted to look and sound like Elvis Presley from the first moment I heard him singing Heartbreak Hotel over a car radio in Waltham Cross.

'n' roll in my heart and a rock band in my sights. I'd discovered that Terry was also crazy about rock 'n' roll, so we decided to break away from the skiffle scene and set up our own rock 'n' roll band. We were fairly confident about getting local bookings, because we were already known around Waltham Cross.

Terry and I recruited Norman Mitham, whom I'd known at school, as guitarist, and we called ourselves the Drifters. Our rehearsal rooms were at Hargreaves Close, that is in the front room of my parents' council house, and that's where I'd be found most evenings at the start of 1958. We would buy or borrow rock n' roll singles each week to add to our regular repertoire of *Blue Suede Shoes*, *Heartbreak Hotel* and *Rock Around The Clock*, and my sister Donna would write down all the words while we worked out the chords.

Our big stage debut came at the annual dinner and dance of the Forty Hill Badminton Club near Enfield. We got the unprecedented fee of ten shillings and loads of applause, which gave a boost to the spirit of our rehearsals. I believe the local council offices still hold records of neighbours' letters of complaint about late-night noise in 1958, and these helped establish a strict 10pm ending to our sessions.

The Drifters played at youth clubs on Fridays and Saturday night dances, then our first 'proper' booking was at the Five Horseshoes pub in Hoddesdon, just north of Cheshunt. It felt like a big break – we were even promised pay! And it was while we were playing there that the Drifters heard those magic words ...

'I can make you a star. I want to be your manager,' said a guy called John Foster.

'Okay, you're on!' we all laughed. It sounded like a big joke and it would be interesting to have a manager. We promised to pay Johnny from our 'silver', as our fee had turned out to be whatever silver was left in the till at the end of the evening, usually a handful of half crowns. And to be sure there was plenty of 'silver' – we'd ask our friends to pay in coins not notes.

John was an enterprising teddy boy by night and a sewage worker by day, but he was determined, burly, at least a year older than us and sufficiently impressed with our act to want to work for us. I owe a lot to Johnny Foster. His conviction that we could be stars was genuine and, even though he was as naive as the Drifters were about the music business, he was absolutely determined to kick-start our careers despite his lack of showbusiness contacts.

His immediate aim was to get us a gig at the famous 2i's coffee bar in London's Old Compton Street. The original owners of the bar, the two Irani brothers (hence its name), had sold it to two flamboyant Australian professional wrestlers, Doctor Death (Paul Lincoln) and 'Rebel' Ray Hunter. Live music was played in the cellar, with the result that young hopefuls came from far and wide in the hope of playing. Tommy Steele was said to have gone into the 2i's basement a merchant seaman and emerged the next morning as a famous musician. Johnny Foster thought we should follow the same route to stardom and within a month, in April 1958, he persuaded Paul Lincoln to give us a two-week booking.

> 'I can make you a star.
> I want to be your manager,'
> said a guy called John Foster.
> 'Okay you're on.' we all laughed.
> It sounded like a big joke...

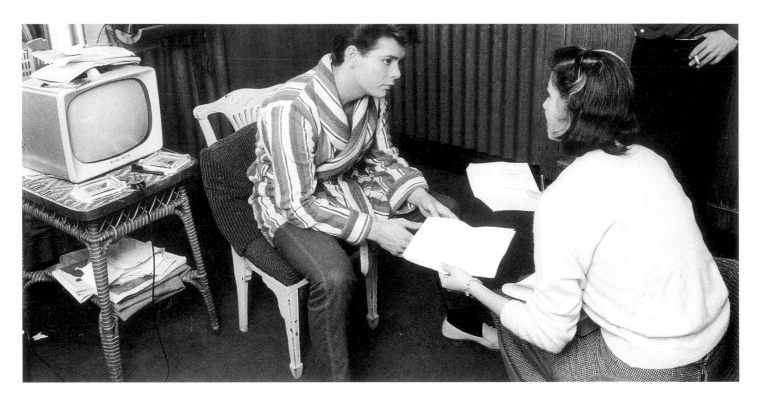

After the release of my first single things began to happen very quickly. Suddenly I was in demand for television and radio – and I loved every minute of it.

Another chance meeting at the Five Horseshoes was with Ian Samwell, a guitarist who was nearing the end of his National Service with the RAF. Somehow he cleverly managed to wangle 'leave' to spend every night in a live music venue. He just came up to our table during an interval at the 2i's and offered his services as a lead guitarist. We accepted his offer without hesitation; it was fairly obvious that the Drifters were lacking bass and lead guitarists and Ian's enthusiastic dedication to rock 'n' roll impressed us all. He soon became a regular at our Hargreaves Close rehearsal room.

When the Drifters went on a group shopping trip in the West End to buy new outfits for the 2i's gigs we all got the same shirt but the band's were all red and mine was white. I'd always wanted to look different from the rest of the band.

I confidently hoped to meet the songwriter Lionel Bart while we were at the 2i's. He had written Tommy Steele's first hit, *Rock With The Caveman* and was said to be a regular in the smokey basement. But no one walked in and made us stars overnight, we met no one particularly famous. The audience were less responsive than our fans at the youth club and we had to spend our fee getting home in cabs (the hour-long bus journey on the 715 bus to central London didn't help, as I suffered from travel sickness), so I was secretly relieved when our 2i's stint was over.

One long-standing contact made at the 2i's was Jane Vane, who had come along with her boyfriend to celebrate her sixteenth birthday. She asked me for my autograph and whether I had a fan club. I just laughed and told her I'd only been playing rock 'n' roll for a few weeks. She said she would start up an official Cliff Richard fan club with six members. She did so and ran it for years, with a membership of 42,000.

Harry Greatorex, a promoter, also saw us at the 2i's and gave us our first out-of-town booking, at a dancehall in Ripley, Derbyshire. He said, 'I'll make sure your name's in big letters – Harry Webb and the Drifters?'

'Oh-oh, no,' I said. 'If you're going to put up my name out front, Harry Webb won't do.'

So we all went off to a nearby Soho pub, The Swiss, and threw around ideas for a name. I took to the idea of Cliff, which clearly has much stronger rock connotations than Harry. Then somebody suggested Richards and Ian Samwell said, 'Why don't you knock off the "s" at the end and that will give you two Christian names – Cliff and Richard. It will be a tribute to Little Richard, too, and when you do interviews people are bound to call you Cliff Richards so you can correct them and your name gets twice the exposure!'

Cliff Richard and the Drifters happily travelled the 150 miles north to perform in Ripley, where we got a great reception from a different type of audience. Our fee was eaten up by the train fare, but we didn't mind sleeping on benches in a corner of the dance hall because the posters had announced in large letters: 'Direct from the famous Soho 2i's Coffee Bar – Cliff Richard and the Drifters'. We had arrived in Ripley!

'I'm Cliff Richard now. What do you think?' I asked my family back in Cheshunt. Dad said, 'All right, Cliff' and from then on that was my name. My youngest sister Joan had trouble with it at first and she'd sometimes say, 'Harry-oh-sorry-Cliff,' as though she had made a mistake, but the whole family accepted my new name instantly and a couple of months later it was in the charts. Sometimes I get a message at the stage door saying a relative has asked for Harry and I know for sure that it's a fan thinking they're being really cute. Nobody calls me Harry.

Johnny Foster's next coup was walking straight into the Gaumont Cinema in Shepherd's Bush when he read a poster outside advertising a talent contest on the last Saturday morning of every month. He found the manager and said, 'Look, I've got a band. They're too good to be in the talent competition but they'll top the bill for free.' Great idea, Johnny.

The management agreed to his something-for-nothing offer and didn't regret their decision. We knew that a lot hinged on our performance at the Gaumont: we were to close the show in a London theatre with a packed audience who would be watching us, not occasionally glancing up from their cups of coffee in the 2i's or pints at the Horseshoes! It didn't matter to us that we'd be performing on a Saturday morning and the audience consisted mainly of youngsters. This was a fantastic opportunity.

All the talent competition contestants went on, introduced by Carroll Levis, then the winner was chosen, and finally we came out as the star-billed band ... and absolutely tore up the audience.

My fans have always been most important to me. My aim is to please them and they have rewarded me with fantastic loyalty throughout my career.

We knew that the screaming fans at the Gaumont Theatre, Shepherd's Bush meant the start of something big. Little did I know that soon I'd be greeted by crowds all over the world.

As we belted out our favourite Elvis and Jerry Lee Lewis numbers, the response was fantastic. With each song the girls went wilder and wilder. They must have been dancing on the cinema seats. It was the first time I'd ever heard screaming. And I loved it!

To see and feel all that response was a fantastic new experience, an exhilarating shock. At the end of our set the stage was mobbed and we literally had to run away from the building to escape. We hared along the road and dived around a corner to hide out of sight – just to be safe from all those screaming girls in hot pursuit. There really would have been no point in trying to stop for a chat!

That experience whetted our appetites. All that screaming told us that something amazing was happening. This was proof to us that rock 'n' roll was not only popular with a little clique; we now had an even stronger feeling that the whole world might enjoy it as much as we did.

Our second booking at the Gaumont the following month could really make our name.

Meanwhile Johnny Foster was determined that we should make a record. He persuaded his own parents to help us with the cost of a basic recording – we cut our first demo disc at the HMV store in Oxford Street. All our instruments were plugged in to the same amplifier and we gave it our all with *Lawdy Miss Clawdy*, and *Breathless*. As soon as Johnny got hold of the disc he disappeared with it, promising to place it in 'the right hands'.

One record company told Johnny that I would never be a singer in a thousand years, but he didn't tell me about that one at the time.

Johnny arranged for an agent, George Gangou, to come along with him to our next gig at the Gaumont, but when I saw the dark suited and booted George Ganjou standing among the screaming teenage girls, his face screwed up in distaste and displeasure, he appeared a most unlikely contact to help further our careers. Nearly sixty and with a strong dislike of rock 'n' roll, George had become an agent after making a living as part of the cabaret act, Ganjou Brothers and Juanita.

Johnny Foster had found us an agent who was an expert in jugglers and operatic singers! Nevertheless, we were relieved

to talk to him after the show and learn that he was very impressed by the riotous reception we received. The following week he took the record we'd made to Norrie Paramor, an established A&R man with EMI.

We heard later from Norrie that George had taken him two records – one by an opera singer which he'd played first and didn't interest Norrie, who told George he had a lot of singers like that. Then, at the last minute, George seemed to remember something else: 'Oh, I've got this record as well. This is something different.'

Thank goodness he remembered. Norrie played our HMV recording while George, I imagine, resisted the temptation to put his fingers in his ears.

'I'd like to hear more from these people,' Norrie told George. On the strength of that £5 recording we were called in to do the audition in Norrie's office and then to record in Studio 2. It was a studio where I was to spend a large part of my life over the next twenty years.

I signed my first recording contract with Columbia, EMI on August 9, 1958. We turned professional on August 5, 1958 and the release date for our first record was fixed for August 29. The day jobs had to go, so I immediately gave in my notice at Atlas Lamps – my polite boss showing only a hint of relief – and Cliff and the Drifters took nine weeks' work at Butlin's holiday camp in Clacton-on-Sea.

Our short season at Butlin's was not without dramas. We arrived to discover that the management wanted us to wear the Butlin's red blazer, as did all the redcoats in the entertainment section.

'We're not wearing those! We can't be redcoats,' said Cliff and the Drifters. We weren't particularly conceited, but we knew that, as stage performers, we wanted to be instantly recognisable. We were eventually found a 'uniform' of white short-sleeved shirts with a big red V on the front.

Our next hurdle was to find a way of playing in the Rock 'n' Roll Ballroom, as opposed the Calypso Room (featuring a Hawaiian band) which was first suggested as our venue. After the Calypso Room we were transferred to the Pig And Whistle pub, whose clientele broke enough chairs to move the management to transfer us to the Rock 'n' Roll Ballroom at last. The half-hour stint in the morning was a nightmare but the evening shows went down well. After a few teething troubles we settled into a routine, like being on

We rock 'n' rollers wouldn't be redcoats at Butlin's in Clacton, so we refused to wear the red blazers, opting instead for these neat shirts.

Hank Marvin was the perfect choice for our new lead guitarist. On our first tour he was in big demand as rival stars asked him to accompany them, too!

holiday with pay. We even got doughnuts and Horlicks for breakfast. What a life!

Norman Mitham decided to leave the Drifters, but we reformed quite smoothly when we were introduced to Ken Pavey, a guitarist already working at Butlin's. He joined us to play lead, and Ian Samwell moved to bass guitar.

We might have been little stars in the audience's eyes while they were on holiday, but we never quite felt that we'd made it because at the end of each week we went back to being non-entities again, as a new intake of campers arrived with their suitcases and we hoped we could impress them.

The first time I heard *Move It* played on any kind of public system was on the radio station at Butlin's. The DJ Tulah Tuke gave us a plug: 'That was the new record from Cliff and the Drifters. You can see them live tonight at the Rock 'n' Roll Ballroom.' We ran over to the radio room and asked her to play it again.

Apart from that the release date of our first record passed quite normally, no overnight record-breaking sales, no glowing reviews, and for a week or so I was contemplating buying a map of the British Isles to swot up on my regional town names for the job back at Atlas Lamps.

Back in Cheshunt Johnny Foster banged on the door and interrupted our rehearsal with some great news: 'Guess what! You're booked on a tour!'

He was whooping, and breathless with excitement. 'Guess the pay!'

'Fifty pounds a week?' I made a wildly optimistic guess. Until then our top fee had been £15. 'Four times that!' Johnny beamed. Two hundred pounds a week was cause for a party.

George Ganjou had come up with a gem of a booking – we were to take part in a full-scale variety show tour in October, with the Kalin Twins, who were visiting from the States promoting their number one hit *When*. The Drifters and I looked at each other and knew we were all thinking the same thing. We needed a bigger line up and more talented musicians for that kind of show, Ken Pavey decided against the tour and I had been advised to leave aside rhythm guitar to concentrate on singing and moving as a front man. So we were on the lookout for a new lead guitarist and another rhythm guitarist.

That's when Hank Marvin and Bruce Welch stepped into the picture. Johnny Foster recommended a young Geordie guitarist he'd met at the 2i's. 'He looks like Buddy Holly and plays like James Burton, Ricky Nelson's guitarist,' he enthused. 'And I bet he'll be willing to join the Drifters if his friend Bruce can come along too. I'd say yes. Bruce plays rhythm guitar and you need plenty of that!'

Hank had played for a while with a skiffle group called the Vipers, led by Wally Whyton. Johnny and I met him and Bruce in London and took them back for an audition at Hargreaves Close, which very quickly turned into a rehearsal for the Kalin Twins tour. The Drifters' line-up became Hank B Marvin on lead guitar, Bruce Welch on rhythm guitar, Ian Samwell on bass and Terry Smart on drums. No one minded that Hank got paid three times for that tour – he was in big demand and had also been asked to help accompany the Most Brothers and the Kalin Twins.

There were about eight acts in the show, chosen as a package to build up to the star turn of the Kalin Twins. Cliff and the Drifters were put on just before the Kalins, obviously considered newcomers who would pose no threat of competition. Little did they know ... As things turned out we got very little experience of playing support.

That tour was my first experience of the hard edge of showbusiness. As the tour began, *When*, the Kalin Twins' current record, was number one in the charts. Then, as it slipped down from its number one slot, my record slowly crept up into second place and the Kalins fell to ninth position.

I remember my eighteenth birthday well... the audience threw flowers on to the stage and everyone stood up to sing Happy Birthday. This was my first tour, my first record was an undreamed-of success – it was an occasion to make a cool and quiffed eighteen-year-old feel very emotional.

The *Oh Boy!* television shows were causing big waves. The horrified reviews didn't bother me — I was busy enjoying the humour of all the luminous socks sent to me from my new fans, until I had a mountain that it would have been impossible to wear in a luminous lifetime!

Even better, I enjoyed the effect of *Move It*'s success on our spot in the Kalin Twins' tour. Cliff and the Drifters stopped the show every night as the new stars of the charts. And from then on the Kalin Twins had to start singing over chants of 'We want Cliff.'

The show's promoters were quick to congratulate me and equally quick to come up with the question, 'Well, Cliff, would you mind coming on earlier in the show so we can get all the screaming over with?'

I refused: 'No, my contract said this is where I go on.' We wouldn't budge. I may have been inexperienced but I knew we were in a great position. We stayed in our slot as the penultimate set and got all the headlines as the English pop stars the Kalin Twins couldn't follow. Harold and Herbert Kalin weren't exactly calling me Mr Nice Guy on that tour. However, there would have been no use in being weak. I'd fought for that position; I wasn't being unfair because that's where I'd been commissioned to play and I also knew instinctively that I had to take advantage of every piece of good timing that came my way. It was the promoters' decision to put me on stage before the Kalin Twins, not my choice, and it worked very well for record sales. I have apologised to Herby and Hal.

The tour had been a great financial success and before it was over the promoter, Arthur Howes, had plans for more tours — this time with Cliff Richard and the Drifters top of the bill.

The only sad note of the tour was when thieves broke into the dressing rooms and stole many valuable instruments, including my very first £27 guitar.

I remember my eighteenth birthday well. It was towards the end of the Kalin Twins' tour and we were playing the De Montfort Hall in Leicester. The audience threw flowers on to the stage and everyone stood up to sing *Happy Birthday*. This was my first tour, my first record was an undreamed-of success — it was an occasion to make a cool and quiffed eighteen-year-old feel very emotional.

Not a hair out of place. Last minute coaxing of the quiff before going on stage.

Life was a merry-go-round. During the course of the tour, the Most Brothers lent us their bass player, Jet Harris and, when Ian Samwell left the Drifters to concentrate on songwriting, Jet joined us. Franklin Boyd became my business manager and John Foster continued to work as my personal manager.

In November 1958 *Move It* was still high in the charts when a follow-up single was released — *High Class Baby*, with *My Feet Hit The Ground* as the B-side, both by Ian Samwell. I broke down and wept as soon as I got home after we recorded *High Class Baby*. The

Drifters line-up was now Jet, Hank, Bruce and Terry and we had done our best for the song but to my ears it sounded very tame and British in comparison to the type of sound we had established with *Move It*. Of course, I was glad when the record got into the charts and peaked at number seven, but the recording has never been one of my personal favourites.

It was around this time that a film company approached Norrie for an up-and-coming singer to appear in a film. It was a black-and-white B-feature movie called *Serious Charge* which was to have a huge hit song in it.

At the beginning of 1959 I was appearing at the Free Trade Hall in Manchester in a show compered by 'a sensational new comedian from Liverpool' – Jimmy Tarbuck. On the bill with us were Tony Crombie and His Rockets and singer Wee Willie Harris. At the end of our last set, with just two more numbers to get through, my voice went on strike. I was moving my lips but no sound came out. There was nothing for it but to ask Wee Willie Harris to stand in the wings and sing the words of my songs while I mimed. It worked very well!

On-stage Wee Willie Harris wore larger-than-life clothes and had flaming orange hair, but it was no surprise to me that the off-stage Wee Willie was a normal, quiet guy and only too happy to help out when my voice disappeared. At that point in the performance I think the audience was rocking so much that no one seemed to notice any change in my voice!

I was relieved that the show had gone well, but I also took it as a serious signal for me – I had my limits and had overstretched my voice, which was a frightening feeling. I'd been working for many weeks and right through Christmas without a break, staying most nights at a flat in Marylebone High Street that I'd rented with John Foster and the Drifters for £18 a week as a convenient London base to avoid travelling miles home in different directions after long recording sessions or gigs. In one week shortly before Christmas 1958 I rehearsed for an edition of *Oh Boy!*, then for another television show, then did some filming for *Serious Charge*, then zoomed off to do two shows each evening at the Finsbury Park Empire.

As soon as I got back to London I went home to sleep a lot and recuperate, knowing I risked burn-out without a more realistic work schedule. I was grateful for the peace and quiet of home and happy for my father to appoint a new manager called Tito Burns. Tito managed the South African-born organ player Cherry Wainer, who became a friend of mine when we worked together on *Oh Boy!* and had recommended him to me.

My father and I were a little wary at first, when Tito spoke about expanding my career beyond what he saw to be the 'constraints' of rock 'n' roll. If I was to appear on established shows like *Sunday Night At The London Palladium*, Tito said he wanted me to use that exposure to entertain all generations of viewers, to be appreciated and accepted by parents as well as teenagers. At first I resisted his ambitions for me as a separate entity from the Drifters because I regarded myself as one of the group, but I could see his point. I would have to

I enjoyed my first car, a grey Sunbeam Alpine with red leather seats – very rock 'n' roll!

spend long hours in the Abbey Road studios recording over the next few weeks, and I knew I needed a manager who better understood the needs of a young rock 'n' roller.

Well rested and raring to go, I was particularly pleased with the results of my next recording stint at Abbey Road. In February 1959, *Living Lovin' Doll*, *Mean Streak* and *Never Mind* were all recorded at the same session. For all those songs Hank had a tiny guitar that we called The Plank because it looked as if it had been cut out of a stump of wood. He must have had a terrible time playing it – the strings were really heavy gauge so it was almost impossible to bend notes, but the result was a distinctive twanging sound. In April 1959 , while we were playing in Birmingham, Hank and I got hold of a Fender Instruments catalogue and sent off for a bright pink Stratocaster. It was the first Stratocaster to be bought in Britain.

At the same time I treated myself to a new Lambretta motor scooter sprayed nasturtium. I didn't get around to choosing my next vehicle until August 1959 – a grey Sunbeam Alpine with red leather seats.

Terry Smart had decided to leave the Drifters (he eventually joined the Merchant Navy) and Tony Meehan became the Shadows' new drummer. Jet Harris recommended Tony, who had backed Adam Faith and Vince Eager and played with the Worried Men skiffle group and Vince Taylor and the Vipers.

For my first album Norrie Paramor executed a daring and dangerous recording plan. After seeing the audience response at live shows, he wanted to produce the album in an innovative way to capture the excitement of a live performance while keeping the technical control of a recording studio. He had a stage built within sight of his control room in studio 2, invited more than 300 people from my fan club, gave them a buffet, then let them into the studio to watch us do the final takes on stage.

We'd rehearsed all the numbers and planned to do the final recordings over two evenings in front of the live audience, but there was rather more 'authentic atmosphere' than we'd bargained for. On the first night the barriers to keep back the fans were set too close to the stage, so too much screaming was picked up on our microphones. Then on the second night I was suffering from a bout of laryngitis and sounded a bit croaky on the recording. But there was no second chance. We couldn't re-book the food and fans and rebuild the stage at the Abbey Road studios, and so my first album undoubtedly has too much screaming in some places and too much croakiness in others.

That debut album was cryptically entitled *Cliff* and if I listen to it now it would be embarrassingly easy to criticize most of the tracks. The first few numbers – *Apron Strings*, two Ricky Nelson numbers *My Babe* and *I Got A Feeling*, Jerry Lee Lewis's *Down The Line* all rock along at a solid pace. Then Jet Harris puts in some nimble guitar on the instrumental *Jet Black*. By the end of the first side, however, my voice sounds as if my tonsils are begging for peace and quiet, and on the second side there are crescendos of screaming which completely drown out the vocals. Nevertheless, I can still listen to the whole album for the sheer

This photo may look as if I'm organising my life, but since my first number one hit I have had to rely heavily on other people to keep my diary and take care of the paperwork.

enjoyment of re-living the experience and knowing that this was the first made-in-Britain rock 'n' roll album recorded live with no overdubbing, and as such it set a new standard. People didn't seem to notice the flaws. Few bands of that era were advised to release a live album in the early part of their careers – the only live Beatles LP was released some years after the group split up and the Rolling Stones' first live EP was mostly inaudible because audience screams were too loud on the recording.

The *Cliff* album was released in April 1959 and reached fourth place in the album charts, while the TV soundtrack album of *Oh Boy!*, on which I sang on seven tracks, made less of an impression on the charts.

In May my fourth single *Mean Streak* was followed into the charts by the other side – *Never Mind* – and my first movie *Serious Change* was released. The character I played was called Curly. There were mornings when, contemplating the long and painful procedure of having my hair curled with hot tongs, I wished I'd tried harder to persuade them to change Curly's name before filming started. But what the heck – having my hair curled before each shoot was a small sacrifice when I was getting the opportunity of singing in a full-scale movie.

When I first walked on to the set of *Serious Charge* it was quite terrifying. I found it difficult to walk onto a stark film set and react to strange people as if they were friends of mine in the story.

They called me a natural actor, which just means I was good at playing myself. The only previous acting experience I had was in the school drama society – as Ratty in *Toad Of Toad Hall* and Bob Cratchit in Dickens's *A Christmas*

> When I first walked on to the set of Serious Charge it was quite terrifying. I found it difficult to walk onto a stark film set and react to strange people as if they were friends of mine in the story.
>
> *Cliff*

ANTHONY
SARAH
CHURCHILL

with IRENE BROWNE, PERCY HERBERT, NOE

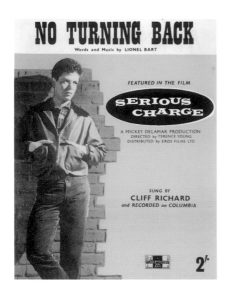

Carol. Something learned from my inspiring English teacher Jay Norris must have stuck in my mind, because somehow I got away with my first film.

My role was as the brother of the reckless leader of a small-town gang, played by Andrew Ray (the son of comedian Ted Ray). Andrew's character was involved in a drama of mutual loathing with the local vicar, played by Anthony Quayle. The cast also included Sarah Churchill, Irene Brown and Percy Herbert, and my part was very minor. Producer Michael Delamar and director Terence Young allowed me to sing three songs backed by the Drifters, and when the best song in the film, *Living Doll* written by Lionel Bart, became a number one hit and people went to see the movie to see me sing it. In the cinema, however, they heard a very different version from the one I'd released as a single.

Living Doll had a slightly troubled start. Even though I'd hankered after meeting Lionel Bart in the 2i's a year before, when I did get to sing one of his songs I hated it. Lionel had first written *Living Doll* as a light love song, inspired by a small advertisement in the *Sunday Pictorial* newspaper: 'She Kneels, Walks Sits and Sings – the Darling Doll' was being sold for 99s 6d or by hire purchase at 8s 6d a week. To work with the theme of the film the song had to be given a rock 'n' roll rhythm, and the result fell between two stools of hot rhythm and gentle romance.

The Drifters and I loathed *Living Doll* at first. We thought of it as pseudo-rock and didn't like the boogie-type tempo. We recorded the soundtrack for *Serious Charge* in April 1958, and when we said we had no desire to record *Living Doll* separately, Norrie quickly pointed out that the small print on the film contract said that a single had to be made ... so we had to find a way.

We were sitting around the dressing rooms at Sheffield City Hall one evening when Bruce Welch started strumming through *Living Doll* in a slow and lazy way, taking out all the boogie-ness, as if to make it sound as plain and boring as possible. He played around with the chords for a while and then said, 'That's it. Why don't we do it as a country song?'

And that's what saved *Living Doll*. We recorded it with as much enthusiasm as we could muster, but it took us a long time to love it.

The first time we had any inkling that it might be a hit was when someone came up to my dressing room with a newspaper, saying 'Look at the chart!' I remember being very pleasantly surprised. We'd entered the Top Twenty at number 14, which was a higher first placing than we'd ever had before. We knew it was going to be a hit then, and we started to like the song more and more as it climbed the charts!

Hank had put in his usually immaculate guitar solo which lifted the track into something different. In those days a guitar solo was regarded as an integral part of the song – when you made a record with a certain guitar solo, anyone else who sang the song would play the same solo. Buddy Holly's solos and Ricky Nelson's solos were thought-out, melodic sequences – not ad libs – and Hank worked that way, too. In my opinion, *Living Doll* was a good record with number-one hit appeal because of Hank's fantastic solo. In fact

In my second film I played the role of Bongo Herbert. This time I was nervous, but my co-stars were incredibly supportive.

Expresso Bongo was great fun to make – and a good film. It was popular in the States where I had a cult following, which meant I got recognised as a film star rather than a singer in America.

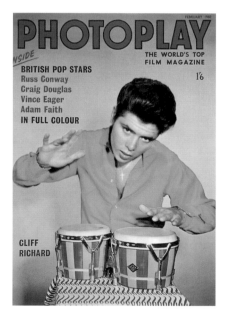

it stayed in the number-one slot for six weeks and became the longest running number one of the year, selling over a million copies and reaching number 30 in the American charts.

It was about this time that the Drifters became the Shadows, and when *Living Doll* entered the charts, Lionel Bart kindly said, 'I think Cliff and the Shadows' unique rendition of my *Living Doll* is merely a rung on the ladder towards better things.'

In my next film I had a few more lines. It was a Val Guest production adapted from a stage play, with a screenplay by Wolf Mankowitz, and entitled *Expresso Bongo*. It's a hoot, a good film and a fifties timepiece, which had an arthouse cult following in the States (where I still get recognised more for that film than for anything else).

This time curly hair was not stipulated in my role as an up-and-coming rock star. My character had the enigmatic name of Bongo Herbert. It was an interesting part to play because Bongo's experience was completely outside my own experience in the music business. Bongo has to deal with a percentage-grabbing manager (Laurence Harvey) and a determined seductress played by Yolande Donlan, cast as a manipulative, fading star. The young rock star eventually ditches the conniving hangers on when he is forced to grow up fast and start asking questions like, 'What am I going to do when I hit twenty?'

When I first walked on to the set of *Expresso Bongo* I thought, 'I'm never going to be able to do this. I'll probably hold up the filming, and all these famous actors are going to wipe the floor with me!'

I'd been told to be careful because actors are out to upstage each other, but I never met with anything but patience and consideration. Laurence Harvey was wonderfully helpful. I remember one scene at a rifle range in an amusement arcade, where I was finding it difficult to think about shooting the rifle and speaking at the same time. After the first couple of rehearsals, Laurence took me aside and explained, step-by-step, the best way of timing the shot and then delivering my line.

Filming with such professionals was perfect groundwork for the films in which I was to star later, and I learned one very important principle that I've used right through my career: if I want to look good on stage then everyone else has to look good. I've seen shows where the support band don't use the same lighting and sound system as the stars and end up looking rather drab in a corner of the stage, with the audience yawning and waiting for the stars. But an audience should expect to enjoy every single part of the show, then they'll enjoy the whole experience much more.

If American singers had a hit record they would quickly follow it with another one that sounded very familiar. And that's how *Travellin' Light* came to follow *Living Doll*. I have to admit that when we went into the studio to record *Travellin' Light* we were thinking, 'Let's do it like the last hit.' I think the success of *Living Doll* had taken us by surprise and we wanted to give a similar treatment to a song we liked better in the first place.

Travellin' Light was written by American songwriters Sid Tepper and Roy Bennett, who had composed many songs recorded by Elvis. It has a badang-dang-chang sound – similar to that in *Living Doll* – with a different tempo and no guitar solo, but nevertheless in the same mould as *Living Doll*. And it worked because it became a number one. But that's the one and only time I actually went into the studio with the idea of recording something that sounded like the previous hit.

Filming with such professionals was perfect groundwork for the films in which I was to star later, and I learned one very important principle that I've used right through my career: if I want to look good on stage then everyone else has to look good.

The teenagers of the day bought singles and, more rarely, albums. But fortunately my second album – released in November 1959 and cunningly entitled *Cliff Sings* – reached number two and produced sales figures that suggested my fans would change their record-buying habits in my case. Norrie was keen to appeal to some of the parents who had bought the single *Living Doll*. I agreed with his decision to give my second album a broader appeal than pure rock 'n' roll, which in those days was still the kind of music that few self-respecting parents would listen to from choice. Half the album was high-voltage rock 'n' roll and the other half was gentle ballads with orchestral arrangements by Norrie Paramor. The album showed I could do something different and benefitted from Norrie's approach of trying fresh ideas. We saw no problem in offering the sound of strings alongside some of our best American rock 'n' roll material.

After all the planes, trains and automobiles on tours all round the world, you'd have thought my body would have become used to travelling, but I still suffer from travel sickness. I was very relieved to get off this plane!

The final recordings of 1959 were the soundtracks for the film *Expresso Bongo* and a number of A- and B-sides ready to take me into the sixties – although at that time I couldn't have envisaged what expansion and acclaim the next decade would bring for British music.

A year after the *NME* dubbed me a crude exhibitionist, it described me as 'the most electrifying talent to emerge in recent years' and gave me a four-page tribute in the September issue of 1959. The following month, *NME* readers voted me Top British Male Singer, and *Living Doll* the Disc Of The Year.

In November 1959 *Expresso Bongo* was released (Winston Churchill attended the première) and I made my Royal Command Performance debut in Manchester before Her Majesty Queen Elizabeth The Queen Mother. I was on the same bill as the Hallé Orchestra, conductor Sir John Barbirolli, and those late, great comedians Tommy Trinder and Arthur Askey.

While I was appearing on the peak-viewing time show *Sunday Night At The London Palladium*, millions of television viewers saw compere Bruce Forsyth walk on stage during my performance, and must have wondered, like me, what was going on.

Bruce grinned at the audience and said, 'Ladies and gentlemen, I just want to announce that Cliff's record *Living Doll* has sold a million.' He pulled out a gold disc he'd been hiding behind his back and presented it to me. I'll always remember that moment because it was our very first gold disc, and it represented a million people choosing to buy one of my singles.

Many people have asked me how I coped with the pressure of such sudden fame at the age of seventeen and eighteen. I always answer that I don't regard fame as a pressure – it was very exciting, but I honestly remember no feeling of pressure. Fame is something you have to deal with and it becomes a problem for those who don't deal with it well because they become badly behaved or overspend. The only pressure of my job is to make a better record, to give a better performance the next time, and for me that was a natural and amazingly fortunate consequence of my wanting to be a singer.

I thank God that I really wanted that acclaim, because otherwise I might have gone the way of many talented people who have suffered a painful demise because they didn't really want the job in the first place. You can get the adulation and the money by being a banker and still sing in the bath, but I had wanted desperately to be a singer. So, to be watched by millions of viewers as I received a gold disc on *Sunday Night At The London Palladium*, two years after I'd left school with few prospects – that did not feel like a pressure, it was just unbelievably exciting!

I really don't think the entertainment industry can be blamed for putting pressure on its stars. Most people do work better under pressure to achieve more, but that pressure comes from within, as a personal challenge. Yes, I wanted to make more hits; I didn't want to be a one-hit wonder. And I'd been welcomed into a world which presented me with the

A signed photo for fans, showing my best impersonation of a moody drummer. This was one of a series of fifty different black and white pictures used for a series of ABC Bubblegum cards in 1961!

possibility of performing in front of thousands of people, on stage, screen and television, with undreamed-of financial renumeration and public adulation. Where is the pressure in that for an nineteen-year-old boy?

To close 1959 the Shadows and I even put rock into pantomime – *Babes in The Wood* at the Globe Theatre, Stockton. It seemed that rock 'n' roll was getting softer edges. I enjoyed singing ballads as well as the more raw rock, and it's true that we were thinking more about appealing to parents too. It would be a few years before teenagers still at school had enough money to buy their own records.

I'd left the normal world at eighteen. I can't understand people who chase fame, enjoy all the benefits, then start complaining. Of course, I complain occasionally, but on the whole I'd rather be where I am than change anything. And I felt more or less the same way as my life steamrollered into the sixties.

✦ ✦ ✦

At the Palladium I appeared with all types of entertainers over a number of years and was proud one year to welcome the legendary Gracie Fields backstage during the panto season.

Singles

1 9 5 8

Move It/Schoolboy Crush

High Class Baby/My Feet Hit The Ground

Livin' Lovin' Doll/Steady With You

1 9 5 9

Mean Streak/Never Mind

Living Doll/Apron Strings

Travellin' Light/Dynamite

Albums

1 9 5 9

Cliff

Cliff Sings

EPs

1 9 5 9

Serious Charge

Cliff No.1

Cliff No.2

Films

1 9 5 9

Serious Charge, Alva Films.

Expresso Bongo, Britannia Films.

Cliff Richard

★ 39

The Sixties

My biggest personal success of
the sixties was going public about
my Christian faith, which gave
my life true meaning – and
even more music! The decade is
remembered as a heyday of pop,
but for a short time I questioned
my place in a recording industry
where faith was bad news and
young lives were ruined by
the linking of sex and drugs
and rock 'n' roll

The Shadows and I were already riding a wave of fame in 1960, as we entered the decade that was to be remembered for an explosion of talent in the music industry. For two years I almost lived on a coach. Travelling overnight from one theatre to another, and each night hoping that my body would one day realise travel sickness was not appropriate to my lifestyle. Every tour was memorable but two of them took me to other continents, which was mind-boggling for a naïve nineteen-year-old.

Our record-breaking TV performance on *Sunday Night At The London Palladium*, which took us into 6,855,000 homes, took place the night before we flew to the States for our first tour of the USA. Four nights later, on January 21, I appeared in *The Pat Boone Show*. This was my first time on American national television and I felt considerably less at ease than I did at the Palladium. Pat Boone described my opening number – *Living Doll* as 'wizard' and 'top-hole', speaking in what Americans of the day perceived as a very English manner. I also sang *Pretty Blue Eyes*, which was introduced as a tribute to Jack Benny.

The following day I swapped my pink jacket for a sharkskin suit and we began the memorable tour, billed as An Added Attraction from Great Britain, in this, '*The Biggest Show of Stars For 1960*'. Top of the bill was Frankie Avalon, who had become a star on Dick Clark's *American Bandstand*, and other leading stars included Freddie Cannon, the Clovers, the Isley Brothers, Johnny and the Hurricanes, Clyde McPhatter and seventeen-year-old Bobby Rydell. Other performers joined the tour in one state and left it in the next.

We were used to travelling around Britain on a Bedford coach, so the Greyhound tour coach, with air-conditioning and reclining seats, seemed luxurious at first. Then, when the winter weather set in and the air-conditioning gave up, we were forced to sleep in overcoats and the Greyhound lost some of its appeal. After each show we moved on to the next venue and we were usually on the road for about eight hours a night, but sometimes 16, with no time for sleep in hotels.

Our first show was in Montreal and the tour continued for 31 consecutive nights, with just four days' rest at the end of February before the last two shows in St Louis and Milwaukee.

Right from the start we got a terrific reaction and the crowds would be screaming for more when we finished our set. We played five numbers, including *Living Doll*, my biggest hit in America, and *A Voice In The Wilderness*, my latest release in the UK. Often no one could follow us on stage until the audience had calmed down. I remember a tall black tour manager who helped make us feel part of the troupe. On our first night he said to the company, 'Well, guys, I think we should all give a big hand to our friends from England for their performance this evening.'

Just before the four-day break in the tour schedule, I had to fly back to England to pick up the very important *New Musical Express* Award at the Empire Pool. I didn't

My first American tour was thrilling, but not very luxurious. We slept on a Greyhound coach for twenty-eight nights and had to wear our overcoats when the winter weather set in!

My mother and father were always very supportive, especially in those hectic early years.

want to miss the awards ceremony, as *NME* readers had been kind enough to vote me Best New Singer in 1959, then promote me to Top British Male Singer in the following year. After a four-hour delay on the flight, I arrived in London at midnight, rehearsed until 4.30 a.m., performed at Wembley in the afternoon and sang at the London Palladium in the evening. I was tired and knew I hadn't given the Palladium my best. Heading back to the States I took my mother to join my father and me.

The tour successfully completed, my only regret was that I had not met Elvis. My parents and I did arrange a meeting with his manager, Colonel Tom Parker, and when we arrived in his office he kindly invited us to join him for lunch. He took out three rounds of sandwiches from his desk drawer and we all tucked in to a wish-you-were-here-Elvis picnic. Unfortunately no arrangements were made for a meeting with Elvis, as Colonel Parker – and the rest of the world – awaited Elvis's discharge from the army before making plans. Elvis was to be discharged from the US army on March 5, 1960, but a meeting was never arranged and I couldn't wait to get back home.

My first single of 1960 was *A Voice In The Wilderness*, written by Norrie Paramor, with *Don't Be Mad At Me* as the B-side. This was my last single in the 78rpm format and it reached number two in the charts. I particularly liked *Don't Be Mad At Me*, for its up-beat bongo drums and a great guitar sequence from Hank. That record was still in the Top Twenty when my next single was released in March. Following the idea tried with *Living Doll*, the A-side was a pop ballad, *Fall In Love With You*, written by Ian Samwell, which reached number two, while the more pacey B-side, *Willie And The Hand Jive*, an American hit for Johnny Otis, registered separately in the charts. We'd all enjoyed listening to the Johnny Otis album and chose *Willie And The Hand Jive* because it was an irresistible dance number, great to do on stage – we choreographed the hand jive so that Hank and Bruce always did a neat one-step turn on the backing vocals.

After the non-stop tour of the States I was looking forward to being back at home and I found time for a little 'housekeeping'. I bought my parents an end-of-row semi at 2 Colne Road in Winchmore Hill, North London. I didn't have much time for choosing home furnishings, but it was great to have the means to furnish a whole house after my parents had struggled for so many years.

Most importantly, it was wonderful to be able to help my parents give up their jobs and live in a comfortable house. It wasn't a huge showbizzy house, but for us it was luxury, with things that we'd only dreamed of owning when we had last moved house.

Soon after the house move I had two appointments with royalty: I was presented to the Duke of Edinburgh at a Leicester Square film première and appeared in a *Royal Variety Performance* before the Queen. The latter appearance was at London's Victoria Palace Theatre, associated for many years with the Crazy Gang who were also in the show. Traditionally a number of comedians appeared on the *Royal Variety* bill, as well as big American stars – Nat King Cole, Sammy Davis Jr and the like. I represented the British pop world with Lonnie Donegan and Adam Faith, in a section of the show called Focus On Youth. We were all to sing with the backing of the orchestra, rather than our regular backing musicians, perhaps because the organisers thought the setting up of amplifiers and equipment would interrupt the smooth running of such a prestigious show.

Glasgow Empire, Blackpool Opera House, Sheffield Lyceum, Bradford's Gaumont and Clacton Essoldo were the venues of a nationwide tour of one-nighters and all seemed relatively local after the epic bus-rides in the States. By the time I'd completed that tour in April my new address had gained such publicity that hordes of sightseeing fans regularly descended on 2 Colne Road, probably to the horror of the neighbours.

My pocket money was raised to £10 a week in September 1960 – it said so in the newspapers – and I treated myself to a red American Thunderbird from Lex Garage in Brewer Street, Soho. Even though I was rarely at home, there seemed little point in parking my car elsewhere because the address had become so well known. Faces appearing at the kitchen window became part of my sisters' washing-up routine, and people would cycle to and fro

Our house in Winchmore Hill wasn't grand, but my parents were delighted to own their own home with all mod cons, including a television set.

> **My family quickly found a way of living with these daily visitations of inquisitive youngsters – we had to put up a large fence which unfortunately became covered in graffiti along the lines of 'Judy was here' and 'I love Cliff'.**

Cliff

to peer straight into the house at all hours of the day. My family quickly found a way of living with these daily visitations of inquisitive youngsters – we had to put up a large fence which unfortunately became covered in graffiti along the lines of 'Judy was here' and 'I love Cliff'. We only lived there for two years, but evidently the house remained something of a tourist attraction for years after we had moved: there was one street in Winchmore Hill whose residents probably wished they'd never heard of me!

In May 1960 Columbia records threw a party for a crowd of teenagers and invited them to help choose my next single from the 24 songs I'd recorded in the previous month. The four most popular were *Please Don't Tease*, *Gee Whiz It's You*, *Nine Times Out Of Ten* and *I'm Willing To Learn*.

They made a good choice – my next single was a number one. *Please Don't Tease*, a lively rock 'n' roll track which made a change from recent gentle ballad-style hits, was written by Bruce Welch and Peter Chester (Peter had led the Five Chesternuts, the group which two years before had included both Bruce and Hank, and had now turned his hand to song-writing). The B-side *Where Is My Heart* was written by Sid Tepper and Roy Bennett, the team who wrote *Travellin' Light*. *Please Don't Tease* became number one in August 1960, but stayed there for only three weeks because it was toppled by *Apache*, the Shadows signature instrumental which established them as recording artists completely in their own right.

While both those records were in the charts the Shadows and I began a six-month season at the London Palladium of *Stars In Your Eyes*, topping the bill with British 50s-style singer Joan Regan, the Canadian singer Edmund Hockridge and top popular pianist Russ Conway. Happily, the Shadows were with me to perform before the Queen Mother in a royal version of the show in December, with Judy Garland, Bruce Forsyth and the Norrie Paramor orchestra.

I was beginning to feel at home at the London Palladium and had grown to love the theatre which had been so awe-inspiring my first time there. But after this long season I vowed never again to spend more than three weeks in one theatre.

It was always a great thrill and an honour to appear on the Royal Variety bill, especially with such great acts as the legendary Crazy Gang.

Cliff Richard

Appearing at the London Palladium meant I had to think about my image. I was going to be seen in 19 million homes and I wanted to entertain the whole family.

My fourth single of 1960 was *Nine Times Out Of Ten/Thinking Of Our Love*. The A-side was co-written by Otis Blackwell, who also co-wrote *All Shook Up* with Elvis Presley, and the B-side was another number written by Bruce and Hank. Our *Me And My Shadows* LP stayed in the top ten of the album chart for more than 23 weeks, but it never got to number one – the soundtrack of the film *South Pacific* was superglued in that spot throughout the autumn.

A ballad entitled *I Love You*, by Bruce Welch, was my next single release and went to number one at the end of the year. The B-side, another Sid Tepper and Roy Bennett number, *'D' In Love*, was also a great song and very popular, but the practice of listing both sides in different chart positions (depending on which song people asked for when they bought the single) had come to an end.

1960 had been a year packed with shows and hit singles. Tito Burns had negotiated a contract with the Grade Organisation for three films with me as the star, so I was looking forward to stepping back into the movie world in 1961, although I never dreamed of a degree of success that would surprised everyone, most of all me.

The director of the first film was to be Sidney J Furie (a respected Canadian director). Peter Myers and Ronnie Cass were commissioned to devise a plot and script, and Herbert Ross, an American choreographer was also employed. I also had my first tour of the Southern Hemisphere booked for spring 1962.

The end of the six-month season at the London Palladium seemed a good time for my first break in 18 months. I had planned the first holiday abroad – to Spain – for my whole family. Unfortunately my father was too ill to come with us. I flew with my mother, two sisters and road manager Mike Conlin. The hotel and good weather offered all the ingredients of a perfect family holiday, but it felt strange to be away from home without my father. We tried to make the most of the long-awaited break, but soon found we all felt the same way and flew home early. The day after Boxing Day Dad had been taken to hospital with a breathing problem and was kept there for a month. I was both moved and comforted by the number of friends who had sent cheery letters and gifts to my father while he was in hospital. He had developed a severe heart condition and, strangely, Dad and I got along a lot better when he was very ill.

My parents' moral standards were still impressed upon me whenever they thought I was keeping bad company or had let them down in some way. After discussion, we appointed Peter Gormley as my manager, a decision I never regretted as Peter became a wonderful mentor and friend to me. He was forty-one then, and had been a journalist, a cinema chain manager and a film director's assistant before he became personal manager in showbusiness. Therefore he knew about publicity as well as making and screening films.

Peter had come to the UK as manager of Frank Ifield, whose records were produced by Norrie Paramor, and that connection led to Norrie inviting Peter to become the Shadows' manager. They had been thriving under his management for six months when Peter and I had our first business conversation in January 1961. Peter did not immediately accept the

I was looking forward to stepping back into the movie world in 1961, although I never dreamed of a degree of success that would surprise everyone, most of all me.

invitation to become my personal manager – he explained that he felt it would be unfair to profit from long-standing arrangements made by his predecessors, but eventually he accepted the job on condition that he didn't earn anything in the first 12 months!

My next single was a ballad called *Theme For A Dream*, with *Mumblin' Mosie* on the B-side. There were advance orders of more than 200,000 and it reached the top three soon after its release in February 1961.

Again I had cause to express my sincere thanks to the readers of the *New Musical Express* who had once more voted me the Top British Male Singer, and the day after collecting that award I set off with the Shadows for a tour of South Africa.

The start of the tour was slow – we were delayed for four and a half hours at London airport. When the flight eventually took off it was six hours late but the long wait had not deterred our welcoming party in South Africa. We were greeted by a 3000-strong pulsating crowd at the airport – I've never had a welcome like it before or since.

The whole route to our hotel was lined with screaming girls and lines of young people trying to catch a glimpse of us. As we neared the hotel in the city centre the crowds were larger, with people crammed together on the pavement, hanging out of office windows, cheering from the rooftops and waving from their shop doorways. A huge banner hung over Eloff Street, where our hotel was, proclaiming, 'Welcome Cliff and the Shadows'. The famous shopping area in the centre of Johannesburg was packed with, according to police estimates, ten to twelve thousand people. It certainly sounded like that many people when they all began chanting, 'We want Cliff, we want Cliff.'

My hotel room had a grand balcony overlooking Eloff Street – the crowd was waiting for me to wave from it! It is very difficult to describe the feeling of looking out at that sea of cheering faces. When I waved, thousands of people as far as the eye could see were waving their arms and fluttering white handkerchiefs. I wanted to wave at every single person in that crowd. One of my most treasured possessions is a black-and-white newsreel, shot by Pathé Cinema News. Occasionally I run it to remind myself of that moment of sheer elation.

Our concert on March 15 at the Johannesburg Coliseum was my first public concert to be recorded live. It sounds naïve now to say that we didn't realise there would be a colour bar controversy over ticket sales for our concerts, but I'm afraid that was the case, so we offered to do two shows especially for the non-Europeans, with the proceeds going to charity.

Back home, our June recording sessions took place in the London studios of Radio Luxembourg and the tapes were broadcast as a 13-week series entitled *Me and My Shadows*. Each show ran for about 15 minutes and featured a lot of the Shadows' own music as well as rock 'n' roll classics.

My father and me at home. When my voice started to show signs of strain from overwork, Dad took on the role of my manager to make sure I didn't overdo it.

Between a Scandinavian tour and opening for a Blackpool season, the Shadows and I began rehearsing for *The Young Ones*, our first Grade Organisation film.

For the first time I was the star of a film and I benefited enormously from working with an actor with the breadth of experience of Robert Morley. As with my first film, people warned me about the difficulties of working with well-established actors. I was advised to be particularly careful not to test the patience of Robert Morley because he did not suffer fools gladly.

Consequently I was so nervous when I did my first scene with him that I completely messed up a couple of lines, necessitating a time-consuming re-shoot. But before I could find the words to apologise, Robert said, 'I'm awfully sorry, Cliff, you'll have to excuse an old dodderer like me but I've made a mistake.'

It was clearly my fault, and so very generous of him to take the blame. I merited no respect as an actor, but I never forgot his thoughtfulness for me as a person.

Robert played a millionaire property dealer who agrees not to demolish a Paddington Youth Club if its members can raise £1500 in ten days to renew the lease on the premises. I

The whole route was lined with screaming girls and lines of young people trying to catch a glimpse of us. As we neared the hotel in the city centre the crowds were larger, with people crammed together on the pavement, hanging out of office windows, cheering from the rooftops and waving from their shop doorways.

play the millionaire's son, whose friends are unaware of the identity of his father and whose father has no idea he is a leading light in the Club. With my youth-club cohorts, Richard O'Sullivan and Melvyn Hayes, I stage a variety show to raise the money, and everyone lives happily ever after.

Making *The Young Ones* was a top-speed learning curve for me and I was grateful for the great spirit of camaraderie between the members of the cast and crew. When the rushes came out of the first three or four days' filming, the whole studio seemed to gain a bit of electric excitement because everyone sensed the film's big potential. A few thousand pounds extra suddenly appeared on the budget sheets, but still I don't think anybody expected this film to be the box-office hit of the year.

All the filming was done in Elstree studios except for a music-hall sequence which was filmed on the stage of the derelict Finsbury Park Empire. A few weeks later the theatre was to be demolished, so there was a little sadness about creating a genuine music-hall atmosphere there, probably for the last time. We used the ragged old curtains, dusted off the lights, filled the auditorium with people, and instantly had the magical Vaudeville atmosphere that would have taken months to recreate in a film studio.

Meanwhile my next single became the tenth of fourteen singles released to attract sales of more than 250,000 and earned another silver disc. It was *A Girl Like You*, written by Jerry Lordan, and on the B-side a livelier *Now's The Time*. I seem to remember it was the first record we had made that didn't have even the slightest mistake on it. Most of our records included little mistakes that we could hear, or perhaps just phrases we knew we could make sound better. *Living Doll*, for example, had a very successful mistake that Hank instinctively corrected so brilliantly that it became part of the pattern of the music. So the mistake-free *A Girl Like You* was quite an achievement, bearing in mind that in those days the recordings were live, with the Shadows playing at the same time as I sang and no overdubbing or splicing together the best-sounding lines.

At the end of a summer season at Blackpool, at the Opera House, we released a part-rock, part-ballad album called *21 Today* – on my 21st birthday, October 14, 1961. The LP was my first to

I was so nervous for the first scene of The Young Ones that I completely messed up my lines, but Robert Morley kindly came to my rescue.

make number one in the album charts, oddly enough taking over from the Shadows' first LP which had held the top place for five weeks. At a party held at EMI headquarters, Sir Joseph Lockwood, the head of EMI, presented me with a camera and a gold disc for sales of more than 250,000 albums. The camera came in useful in Australia, where we headed on tour straight after my birthday party.

Visiting Australia for the first time was the perfect birthday treat, and I've loved the country ever since. We played to 12,000 people each night, in Sydney, Melbourne, Perth, Adelaide, then on to New Zealand – which involved 28 different flights between venues.

These days I always try make sure I work there when it's winter in the UK! I tour Europe in the winter, too, and the audiences are fantastic. But wintertime is not the best

ASSOCIATED BRITISH Presents
starring
CLIFF RICHARD · ROI
IN
"THE YOUNG
WITH
CAROLE GRAY · ROB
MELVYN HAYES AND
A CINEMASCOPE PICTURE
RELEASED BY WARNER-PATHE

season to appreciate the countryside, whereas in Australia I can relax in their summer sunshine, play tennis, swim, sunbathe, take boat trips in Sydney harbour – all of which makes touring there a great pleasure.

When we first went to Australia no one over the age of eighteen liked rock 'n' roll. But yesterday's teenage rockers are today's middle-aged rockers, which is reflected in the audiences at concerts in Australia. I think Europe is becoming far more ageist about rock than Australia, where open-air concerts are something of a tradition for all age groups.

On the first Australian tour Brian Bennett was on drums in place of Tony Meehan who had left the Shadows to work in the A&R department of another record company. It was fortunate that Brian was able to fit into our routines so smoothly and quickly. We had known him from the 2i's circuit, and as part of the Wild Cats who had played with Marty Wilde. The tour was successful but for me it was also a time of reflection of the kind that would lead me to Christianity. Perhaps that is also part of the reason why Australia is a very special place for me – it was there that I began a most important spiritual journey and started to grapple with my ideas about religion and mortality, which are thrown into such sharp focus when one loses a parent.

My father had died in May, the month before his favourite song of mine, *A Girl Like You*, was released, and now, more than ever, I was aware of   and grateful for – the impact of his strict moral code on my own character.

He was stubborn to the last, challenging the doctors' diagnosis, but somehow the final months of his life brought us much closer together. He had been in hospital for two or three weeks, but his death was a sudden and a numbing shock. Although my life went on apace and I was busy being me, I was vaguely ill at ease with myself.

After saying goodbye to the screaming crowds at the Australian concerts I would return to my dressing room and feel like I was sitting in a void. Outwardly everything was the same and I got the same total enjoyment and elation on stage, but afterwards, whether in company or alone, I felt an absolute emptiness. Very faintly an interior voice was saying, 'Please, I'm not quite satisfied...'

I don't know what sparked it off – I wasn't dissatisfied with my career or unhappy about fame, as has been suggested. My success certainly wasn't lonely; I was surrounded by friends, liked the people I worked with, lived with a loving family, and before me lay an array of film, television and recording opportunities. However, I can sense a definite link between my father's death and the beginning of my journey towards being a committed Christian.

Curiosity led me to consider approaching a spirit medium to try to contact my father, who might know what was wrong. Fortunately I never got to a medium because Licorice Locking intervened with the Bible.

Brian Locking – nicknamed Licorice – had taken over from Jet Harris as bass

The Young Ones premièred at the Warner Theatre in London on 13 December 1961. My mother and I flew to South Africa just before Christmas to attend the film's premières in Johannesburg, Cape Town and Durban.

> Visiting Australia for the first time was a perfect 21st birthday present. I've loved the country ever since - audiences are friendly and the summers are long...

player with the Shadows when I casually mentioned that I planned to attend a seance. I thought I knew him quite well but he suddenly became more agitated than I'd ever seen him. He pulled a small Bible out of his jacket pocket and read out verses which expressly forbade any dabbling with spirits and mediums, in a tone of certainty and authority that I had never heard in his voice before. I was amazed that the Bible had anything to say that related to my life. I'd always thought of it in terms of an important and interesting piece of history, but here was Licorice reading out line after line which applied directly to me in the here and now. Although I knew Licorice had religious beliefs, I'd had no idea that he was a Jehovah's Witness.

As a result of that chance revelation I got out my own Bible and began going with Licorice, Hank, and our new drummer Brian Bennett to Jehovah's Witness meetings. I enjoyed being one of a crowd in the anonymous congregation at Kingdom Hall.

The 1961 Australian tour was in that sense a beginning. Six months after my father's death, and with an exciting career still unfolding before me, I began asking the questions which many young people ask. And I was finding quite different answers from those that were about to be represented by the hippie culture. Images of peace bells, love-ins and unnaturally induced states of meditation were just around the corner for the pop industry, but for the next two years Cliff and the Shadows' dressing-room discussion would revolve around the Bible. It wasn't that we weren't ready for Flower Power. We already knew we didn't need it.

We returned from Australia in time for the première of *The Young Ones* in December. The soundtrack album spent six weeks at the top of the LP charts and the film was the second biggest box-office hit of the year, beaten only by *The Guns Of Navarone*.

I think that after *The Young Ones* my image became more accessible – less of a bad boy and more of the boy next door. The film brought mums and dads to the cinema, and I had no problem with them enjoying my records too. My singles were very different from those of 1959, and that set a pattern for my career in that just about every year since then I've tried to experiment with a different sound.

The single of *The Young Ones* entered the charts at number one in 1962. It is the only record I've ever made that was released on a Friday and was number one on the Monday morning. There were advanced sales of more than a million copies and it stayed in the charts for 21 weeks, to become my biggest-selling single so far. It was a very exciting time and the following singles all reached the top four ...

In April 1962 I was awarded a gold disc for *The Young Ones* and the following month *I'm Looking Out The Window/Do You Wanna Dance* became my first double-sided hit, reaching number two in the charts and serving as a clear reminder that I had no intentions of deserting rock 'n' roll.

By the age of 21 I had performed in three continents and gained considerable confidence as an entertainer. I wasn't lonely and I wasn't unhappy about fame, but something sparked off a feeling of dissatisfaction.

Cliff Richard

After waving goodbye to
the screaming crowds, I would
return to my dressing room and
feel as if I was sitting in a void.
I got total elation and enjoyment
on stage, but afterwards
an interior voice was saying,
'Please, I'm not quite
satisfied...'

Cliff

Cliff Richard   ✴ 61

The making of *Summer Holiday* took place in Greece and it was every bit as much fun as it looks in the film. The cast brought together what was to become a friendly group both on – and off-camera – Richard O'Sullivan, Melvin Hayes, Jeremy Bullock and Una Stubbs were a fabulous team that I was proud to be part of. We really were the stars, and the established actors, including Ron Moody and David Kossoff, had character cameo roles.

All the laughs and high spirits in the film are authentic because we really were just a group of young people thrilled at the opportunity to spend six sunny weeks driving a London bus around Greece. In my opinion, the end result was more original and fresher than *The Young Ones*.

One of the film's might-have-beens is that I almost had Barbra Streisand as a co-star. Herbert Ross, the choreographer who also worked on *The Young Ones*, had staged Barbra's first show on Broadway and – not surprisingly – thought she was the bee's knees. Our producer flew to New York to see her and thought she wasn't quite right!

My leading lady was chosen from the Broadway production of *The Sound of Music*. Carole Gray had just married a young American actor by the name of Jon Voight, and was so homesick that she spent all her salary on weekend flights to and from New York.

By now I was getting used to the demands of making a movie. Repeating the same performance again and again, with identical movements so that close-up and long shots can be married together and so on. All that disciplined repetition demands a lot of patience and is physically very tiring. But it's a great feeling when you get it right.

For the filming of *Summer Holiday* I made a real effort to lose weight and have been on a diet ever since. I find that one good meal in the evening and a light snack at lunch time is the only way I can keep off the pounds, and I know I'm eating enough of the right foods because I still have loads of energy and don't get hungry

Right: Me and the Shadows appearing before Princess Margaret and the Bishop of Bath at Eton College Mission's Youth Club in Hamburg. Below: With Janet Munro, Sylvia Sims and Richard Attenborough at the Royal Film Performance of West Side Story *in February 1962.*

Cliff Richard

between meals. The person who really triggered my determination not to gain weight was Minnie Caldwell, one of the original characters of *Coronation Street*. In April 1962 I was watching the show when Minnie, sitting in the park listening to a brass band, said, 'Isn't Cliff Richard a lovely, chubby lad?'

That was it; goodbye chubby-ladishness. That's when I put an end to my Tizer and ice cream habit on tour and stopped nibbling at Indian sweets. By the time I started filming I was down to eleven stone, and since then I have kept to that weight.

My third single of 1962 was *It'll Be Me*, the Jerry Lee Lewis rock 'n' roll classic, written by Jack Clement, with the slower love song as the B-side this time – *Since I Lost You*, written by Hank and Bruce. I chose *It'll Be Me* simply because it was a favourite of mine, and it became a number-two hit.

Most of the songs for *Summer Holiday* were written by the Shadows, with a little help from me or by the scriptwriters Peter Myers and Ronnie Cass. We spent the last weeks of 1962 working on the soundtrack and both sides of the first single, *The Next Time* and *Bachelor Boy*, which made a fantastic Christmas present when it reached the number one spot.

Then *Summer Holiday*, released in February 1963 and my twentieth single, went to number one – twice. The *Summer Holiday* soundtrack LP stayed at the top of the album charts for 14 weeks, during which time I was on a 41-date tour of Britain. My next single, *Lucky Lips*, was written by the legendary American songwriting duo Harry Leiber and Mike Stoller and had been a hit for Ruth Brown and Gale Storm in America some years before. That one has always been a favourite in Germany. It topped the charts in Norway, Israel, South Africa, Hong Kong, Sweden and Holland. In England it reached number four, which was a low placing for me after so many number ones. 1963 was a big year for the Beatles and, while my next three records were all in the top five places in the charts, it was not easy to accept that my string of number ones had come to an end. Ray Coleman in *Melody Maker* wrote that I was, 'facing dangerous days with zest, honesty and fervour ... after five years of glory during which Cliff has established himself as Britain's top solo pop idol, it has been said that the route from now on can only be downhill.' And so it has been said many times!

'All the laughs and high spirits in the Summer Holiday are authentic, because we really were just a group of kids thrilled at the opportunity to spend six sunny weeks driving a double-decker bus around Greece.

Cliff

Before filming started I got my weight down to 11 stone and I've stayed at that weight – give or take a few pounds – ever since. Although three red double-decker buses were bought for Summer Holiday, only one was used. It came from Cricklewood Garage and the code number of the depot can be seen on the side.

ELSTREE DISTRIBUTORS LIMITED present
CLIFF RICHARD · LAURI PETERS
in "SUMMER HOLIDAY" U
with DAVID KOSSOFF
Guest Star RON MOODY and THE SHADOWS
A CINEMASCOPE PICTURE IN TECHNICOLOR
Produced by Kenneth Harper
Released through Warner-Pathe Distributors Ltd

The sales of *Next Time/Bachelor Boy* earned a gold disc, which I received during the 100th edition of ABC Television's *Thank Your Lucky Stars*. Other pop stars on the show, who represented a changing mood in the music business, were Billy J Kramer and the Dakotas, the Searchers and Brian Poole and the Tremeloes. I also had the opportunity to sing my new single, *It's All in The Game*. This wasn't a new song, but was such a beautiful one that I'd wanted to record it for quite a while.

My last single of 1963, *Don't Talk To Him* was described in a music paper as 'a haunting melody in slow cha-cha tempo'. I don't think Bruce had regarded the melody as a cha-cha-cha when he brought it for me to listen to and asked if I could think of a lyric. We were quite pleased with the result and I felt we had a great songwriting team in the making.

By this time, I wanted to buy a family house that I could keep a secret. Neighbours had been unsettled by fans seeking out my last address and I felt it was my responsibility to give my mother and sisters a home with more privacy. I found a six-bedroom Tudor-style home, set in 11 acres in Upper Nazeing but, unfortunately, very soon after we moved in the national

Cliff Richard ★ 67

I love any shots of me that make me look as though I can dance. The pose I'm striking here looks as if I'm about to fall over in the next frame! While we were making the film there was a rumour in Fleet Street that I couldn't dance because I'd been injured in an accident. In fact, a passer-by had seen us filming the scene where Una's old banger got involved in a pile-up with a lorry and reported it as a real accident!

ELSTREE DISTRIBUTORS LIMITED present
CLIFF RICHARD · LAURI PETERS
in **"SUMMER HOLIDAY"** Ⓤ
with **DAVID KOSSOFF**
Guest Star **RON MOODY** and **THE SHADOWS**
A CINEMASCOPE PICTURE IN TECHNICOLOR
Produced by Kenneth Harper
Released through Warner-Pathe Distributors Ltd

press were knocking at the door and groups of fans were loitering outside, even when I was in another country.

The third of the three films contracted by Tito Burns was made in the middle of winter, in the Canary Islands. So we expected echoes of the *Summer Holiday* atmosphere. More sun and fun? Sadly, no.

Celluloid does not lie in this case – *Wonderful Life* was, by any standards, a disaster. The whole project seemed jinxed. The Canary Islands' location was chosen for its sunshine and golden sands but, until we arrived, no one knew that the golden sands turned black as coal in the rain and took four days to dry out. We were there for ten weeks and it rained for ten weeks.

The bad-weather standby scenes formed a 15-minute section of the film called 'The History of the Movies' and that particular part of the film is far better than any of the rest. One brief scene was picked up by the press as being controversial – it was a send-up of the scene in the James Bond film *Dr No*, where Sean Connery encounters Ursula Andress emerging from a tropical lagoon in a revealing bikini. Our 'Ursula' was English rose Susan Hampshire and I was supposed to be James Bond.

One critic said of the film, 'There's everything in this film but the kitchen sink.' It was released in 40 different cities and it took seven years to make any money. The film certainly didn't change anyone's life for the better – except that the proceeds of the première went to the national Association of Youth Clubs.

The new departure of 1964 was a pop pantomime: *Aladdin and His Wonderful Lamp*. The Shadows wrote a musical score and other cast members – Audrey Bayley, Faye Fisher, Joan Palethorpe and Una Stubbs – sang on many of the tracks.

Taken that Beatlemania was now in full flow, I was pleased with the chart performance of my singles. *The Lonely One* was the 1964 new year single, reached the top ten at the same time as *Don't Talk to Him* re-entered the charts. *Constantly*, an adaptation of a traditional Italian hit favourite called *L'Edera* made number three, then *On The Beach*, a great song from *Wonderful Life*, also did well in the charts. *I Could Easily Fall* was taken from the recording of *Aladdin and His Wonderful Lamp* and was already a hit before the pantomime opened at the London Palladium in December. *Angel/Razzle Dazzle* was a track which, in the same way as *Gee Whiz It's You*, and *What'd I Say*, was distributed overseas but found its way into UK record shops.

Norrie decided that we should do some recording in New York and Nashville, just for the experience. We booked sessions for August and included some vocals by the Jordanaires, Elvis Presley's backing group, and worked with the producers Bob Morgan and Billy Sherill. They were very inventive. I remember once when I was sound-testing I asked the sound engineer in my usual manner, 'Am I all right? Am I close enough or would you like me further away?' It was the first time I'd heard a reply of the ilk, 'You're the singer, sing. I'll get it on tape.'

*The gala world première of Summer Holiday
was on 11 January 1963.*

A Celebration

His approach worked, because the sound quality was of a high standard and produced three hits – *On My Word, Wind Me Up* and *The Minute You're Gone*, the latter proving to be my bestselling single of 1965.

The advance booking for our pantomime at the London Palladium topped one million pounds and was the highest in the history of the theatre. Our three-and-a-half month run was great fun – it couldn't fail to be enjoyable, with the nation's favourite comedian, Arthur Askey, playing the Dame and Una Stubbs as the delightful Eve. Each show was interesting, mainly because something different happened during every performance!

The film opened nationally on 18 February and broke all previous box office records for a British film. We always had high hopes for it, but the public response was phenomenal.

Cliff Richard

★ 71

Susan Hampshire and I had worked together previously on Expresso Bongo, which was an altogether happier experience than the making of Wonderful Life! (opposite).

Cliff Richard

At the end of the pantomime run I was voted Top British Singer for the sixth year running by readers of the *New Musical Express*.

The remainder of 1965 had a distinctly international flavour – I'd already recorded the *When In Spain* and *When In Rome* albums and, in October, we flew to Warsaw to play two historic concerts organised by the Polish government. Two days later, on my twenty-fifth birthday, we did two concerts in Beirut, and in the same month we became the first British artists invited to play at the French Film industry's Gala. We appeared at the Paris Marigny Theatre before Princess Grace of Monaco, then did a brief tour of France.

Learning *La Mer* and *Boum* in French wasn't as tricky as *Lucky Lips* and *I'm the Lonely One*, which I had to learn phonetically in German. I'd also been singing a couple of Spanish songs on tour, so altogether I was working in four different languages.

I remember playing at the Paris Olympia and being stunned by the behaviour of the audience – they were so polite! Everyone would sit perfectly still and silent during a song, then suddenly burst in loud and long applause at the end!

Quite a change from the screams we had grown accustomed to!

It was good to work again with Richard O'Sullivan, Melvin Hayes and Una Stubbs, all highly professional and great fun.

In the many spaces between the tours and applause of 1965, I was revelling in significant changes in my circle of friends and my exploration of the Scriptures. Meeting my sister Joan's class teacher, Mr Latham, seemed simply a part of my brotherly duty since our father's death, even though Joan was noticeably keen that I should meet him and not a little starry-eyed about her handsome new form teacher.

And there was another caring influence at play: Jay Norris, my old English teacher, had remained a friend and was sufficiently concerned about my Jehovah's Witness interests to engineer my meeting with the head of religious studies at her school – the same Bill Latham. Jay always celebrated her birthday with a car rally and later admitted that it was no coincidence that I should

find myself a passenger in Bill's car. Much to Jay's disappointment Bill and I had a good chat, enjoyed the rally and also came in as runners-up, but never got around to talking about religion.

Jay didn't give up. A few months later Jay, Bill and Graham Disbrey, another teacher, and I were sitting in my home in Nazeing discussing the Holy Trinity. I stuck stubbornly to my JW platform, although I was impressed by the way they spoke about Jesus. There was an assurance that I'd never heard in Jehovah's Witnesses.

Bill invited me for another chat, this time with David Winter who later joined the BBC as producer of religious programmes, and then asked me if I'd like to sit in on a Sunday afternoon Crusader class. It was difficult to look nonchalant under the gaze of thirty goggling schoolboys, but we all got used to each other after a few weeks and I was accepted as part of the class.

The Crusader approach to evangelical Christian teaching began to make more and more sense to me. Some of my previous misconceptions about Christians were eradicated and most importantly, the idea that different groups of Christians were absolutely divided. Bill was an Anglican, Graham a Baptist and another leader was an elder in a Brethren assembly, yet in their teachings there was no hint of division – they all professed to know the same Jesus whom, they said, was available to me too.

For about a year I was divided between my JW group of friends and the Crusader class, which made for some very interesting, sometimes heated, discussions.

Later my career and my beliefs would exist in tandem, but during this period I'd set myself on a journey of discovery which necessarily took a lot of my energies and, although I did not neglect my professional commitments, I was less preoccupied with showbusiness success than I had been for many years.

The turning point came while I was filming *Finders Keepers* at the Pinewood Studios. I was staying with Bill and his mother at their house in Finchley and one evening I was sitting in my bedroom reading the book of Revelation, where Jesus says, 'Behold, I stand at the door and knock; whoever hears my voice and opens the door, I will come in.' That was God's moment for

The fans followed me everywhere but I never thought of it as a pressure. It was part of the career I'd always dreamed of.

In Finders Keepers, The Shadows and I played five penniless musicians who stow away on a train to Spain.

*Sometimes a nice cup of tea was all
I wanted on the road!*

Cliff Richard ✱ 79

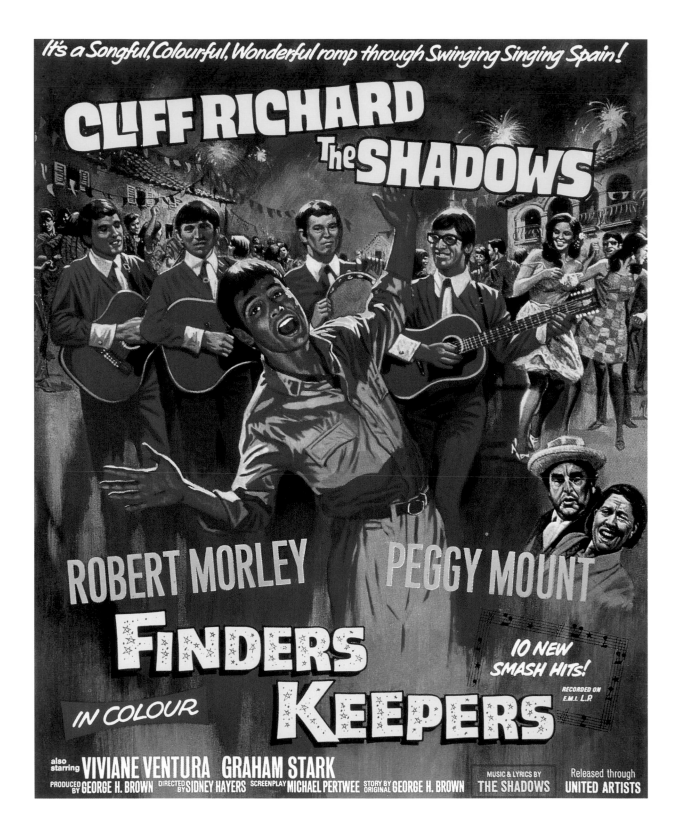

In 1966 Finders Keepers was ranked top musical of the year. Although several locations in the film were photographed in Spain, I never got to go there myself because all my scenes were shot at Pinewood Studios in England. Left: With my mum and Pippa Steele at the Leicester Square première of Finders Keepers on 8 December 1966. Below: Vivian Ventura's sultry South American looks were just right for the part of Amelia in Finders Keepers.

me. There were no flashes of light or sudden sensations. I just mouthed a hesitant prayer, 'All right, Jesus, I know that you are knocking – you'd better come in and take over.' I meant it and I was prepared for the consequences. It was as simple as that. It was not a moment of high emotion but a cool and reasoned conclusion that I needed Jesus.

So there is nothing dramatic to tell about my conversion and, since then, thirty wonderful years of getting to know Him are the evidence that Jesus accepted my simple invitation.

A few months previously I'd not had much idea where Finchley was, but now I needed the encouragement and patience of the Christians I'd met there, and Finchley was to be the focal point for a radical change in my lifestyle.

My family at Nazeing were going their separate ways – my sister Donna was already married, Jacqui was engaged to be married and my mother was also planning to marry. I had no inclination to stay on and rattle around Rookswood on my own and, as none of us had been there long enough to make it feel like a family home, selling the house was not a difficult decision. It so happened that Bill and Mrs Latham were moving house and it seemed an obvious choice to join forces. The three of us had co-existed very happily and Mamie Latham had no objection to her 'second son's' peculiar hours.

My showbusiness life was still very busy. The singles I released in 1966 and 1967 all became chart hits, there were television appearances, concert tours at home and abroad,

and a big success with my international audience was the album *Cliff In Japan*, recorded live in concert. But my attitude toward my career was different – it was important but it was no longer all-important. Crusaders, Bible study nights, Crusader cruises on the Norfolk Broads and summer camps all now held equally important places in my diary.

At around this time I was confirmed as a member of the Church of England at St Paul's Church in Finchley. On Christmas Eve 1966 I took my first Communion, coming home just in time for the midnight service after doing two shows at the Palladium. I had performed to a wonderfully responsive audience in the bright lights of London. Immediately afterwards, taking bread and wine for the first time was a wonderfully spiritual experience and a turning point in my story ...

It was probably through one of the Crusader activities I'd taken part in that other organizations heard about my conversion. I received a few letters from Christian groups wondering if I'd be free to take part in this or that. And somehow Billy Graham must have heard about my non-pop activities because I received a letter inviting me to speak about my faith at a Youth Night during his UK Crusade.

I knew I had to do it and that in terms of making a public stand this was the crunch. I felt certain that newspaper reports would centre on speculation and misunderstandings about my conversion.

I was also very much aware that if my career collapsed I was not much use in any other job. The only work I knew was singing and I was trained for nothing else. While I had found out how to live happily with both showbusiness and my religion, the music business of the sixties was unlikely to take kindly to anyone with unfashionable attitudes, which unfortunately included attitudes of faith. With many more years of experience behind me now, I know that if my career had ended then, or even if it ends tomorrow, I'm confident that God would lead me somewhere else. The more we depend on God the more dependable we find He is.

As I stepped on to the platform at Earl's Court for Billy Graham's Crusade, I experienced a degree of stage fright I had never had to conquer before. It took me ten minutes to say my piece and sing a song, and just remembering it brings me out in a cold sweat. For two years I'd been bursting with happiness at the way Christianity had changed my life, and now I had to express that faith to an audience of 25,000 people. While I spoke I put my arms on a desk in front of me for support and I must have been very tense because when I moved away from the desk to sing I had terrible pins and needles in my arms.

I began singing *It's No Secret* and let my arms hang by my sides, hoping that the pins and needles would quickly disappear, but when I tried to lift an arm in a gesture to emphasise the words of the song, I couldn't move it. Thank goodness I'd decided not to play guitar and was accompanied by Billy Graham's pianist Tedd Smith. I had to sing the whole song with my arms pinned to my sides and returned to my seat walking like a robot!

To add to the tension, my 'performance' was being filmed for the Billy Graham film

I experienced a degree of
stage fright I'd never known before
the first time I spoke about
my faith on Billy Graham's
Crusade platform.

Cliff

Cliff Richard

I welcomed the opportunity to appear in Two A Penny because it was a serious role in a Christian film.

Two A Penny, which I'd also agreed to appear in.

In the film I played a character called Jamie Hopkins who was very cynical and critical of the rally. I carried a set of instruction cards from the director, Jim Collier, and removing a card from my pocket was a signal to the cameraman that I was about to carry out one of Jim's instructions. These went something like, 'Think that all the audience must be woolly-headed sheep', 'Look towards Billy and sneer'. My 'acting' didn't go completely unnoticed, as I received a couple of letters, presumably from people with very good eyesight on the front row, complaining about my appalling behaviour during Billy's sermon.

I welcomed the opportunity to play a serious role in a Christian film with a £150,000 budget where all the proceeds would go to charity. Ironically though Equity, the actors' union, were somehow able to ban me from working for nothing and insisted on a payment of £40 a week before tax! I also knew *Two A Penny* would reach an international audience because there were to be German and Japanese versions made, too. And if that wasn't tempting enough, I was allowed to contribute three songs for the film – *Two A Penny*, *Love You Forever Today* and *Questions*.

I felt ambivalent about taking on the role in *Two A Penny*, but Jim Collier's words at the start of the project made everything crystal clear and reversed my decision to leave showbusiness. 'Why is it that when people get converted they want to leave their jobs and do something different?' he said. 'Our role is to be Christians first and foremost right where we are.'

It had never occurred to me that God might have had a hand in my past as well as my future, and that I already had the career He'd intended.

Three years later I was privileged to work with Jim again, on a documentary-style film, *His Land*, which portrayed modern Israel in the light of ancient prophecies. Jim was the only director I'd ever worked with who encouraged me to think in depth about my character. His sincerity and energy inspired everyone working with him – actors, extras and film crew alike.

From then on I simply had two diaries – one for my Christian activities and one for showbiz. While my manager Peter Gormley, my touring manager David Bryce, and their staff looked after Cliff Richard the singer, Bill became my 'Christian Activities Organiser'. My advice to anyone who feels he or she hasn't progressed much in the Christian life is to get up and do something! I was lucky to have so many invitations to speak about Jesus and to have Bill to help me keep my busy diary, but it taught me how much your faith has a chance to grow when you're involved, and needing to depend on God.

I often think that answering questions from an audience helps me more than it does the audience. I do believe that when we are forced to define an opinion God will give us the right words to say in a difficult situation. David Winter had an idea that I should write down the answers to a few of the questions most commonly asked me and turn them into a book. With this in mind, I wrote *The Way I See It*, which led to two more books,

Questions and *The Way I See It Now*. They have sold in dozens of countries and have even been translated into Hebrew.

Probably my most significant recording achievement of the late sixties was my first album of gospel songs, recorded and released in October 1967. I knew that my *Good News* LP had a limited audience, but as Christianity was now at the centre of my life, I needed to be able to sing about it. The tracks included *The 23rd Psalm*, *When I Survey The Wondrous Cross*, *The King Of Love My Shepherd Is*, *What A Friend We have In Jesus*, and *It's No Secret* (previously recorded by Elvis). A Christian audience was now very important to me and I wanted to be able to record for them as well as the pop fans I'd built up over the years.

The second half of 1967 included some interesting overseas successes – an appearance with the Shadows at a song festival in Split, Yugoslavia, was memorable not least because we did ten curtain calls!

1968 saw an opportunity to represent England in the *Eurovision Song Contest*. I recorded the six songs proposed as our *Song For Europe* and sang them on Cilla Black's television series. The winning number, receiving 171,000 of the 250,000 votes from viewers, was *Congratulations*.

I was disappointed when *Congratulations* came second to *La La La* from Spain's Massiel, but it was no disgrace and our song became a lasting favourite in many countries. Funnily enough, Germany, whose votes lost us the first place in the contest, placed advance orders for 150,000 copies of the record!

It was released in 30 versions around the world and I recorded the song separately for nearly every country in Europe. A month after the contest *Congratulations* was top of the charts in Denmark, Holland, Belgium, Sweden and Norway, and in the top ten in Spain, France, Germany and New Zealand.

As well as becoming my fifth million-selling gold record, *Congratulations* won two Ivor Novello Awards in 1969, one for the most performed work and one for the International Song of the Year.

Established 1958 was my last album with the Shadows. It involved a celebration and a goodbye, commemorating our ten-year association at the time when the Shadows had announced they would be disbanding at the end of 1968. The sleeve notes by Tim Rice (then working for EMI) suggested that we would still be together in another ten years' time when Elvis would be forty-three. Sadly neither of these things were to happen. The Shadows bowed out of the chart scene on a high note – they had written every track on *Established 1958* and their distinctive instrumental style would never be successfully imitated.

As well as becoming my fifth million-selling gold record, Congratulations won two Ivor Novello Awards in 1969, one for the most performed work and one for the International Song of the Year.

With my sister Donna admiring Lady
Penelope and Parker at the premiere of
Thunderbirds Are Go in 1966. The Shadows
and I featured in the film in puppet form.
The instrumental Lady Penelope was played
by the puppet Shadows on the stage of the
Swinging Star night club, then puppet Cliff
Richard Junior was introduced as 'the
biggest star in the universe' and sang
Shooting Star. Posters advertising the film
warned 'adults over sixteen should be
accompanied by children'.

singles

1960

A Voice In The Wilderness/Don't Be Mad At Me

Fall In Love With You/Willie And The Hand Jive

Please Don't Tease/Where Is My Heart?

Nine Time Out Of Ten/Thinking Of Our Love

I Love You/In Love

1961

Theme For A Dream/ Mumblin' Mosie

Gee Whiz It's You/I Cannot Find A True Love

A Girl Like You/Now's The Time To Fall In Love

When The Girl In Your Arms (Is The Girl In Your Heart)/Got A Funny Feeling

What'd I Say/Blue Moon

1962

The Young Ones/We Say Yeah

I'm Looking Out The Window/Do You Wanna Dance

It'd Be Me/Since I Lost You

The Next Time/Bachelor Boy

1963

Summer Holiday/Dancing Shoes

Lucky Lips/I Wonder

It's All In The Game/Your Eyes Tell On You

Don't Talk To Him/Say You're Mine.

1964

I'm The Lonely One/Watch What You Do

With My Baby

Constantly/True True Lovin'

On The Beach/A Matter Of Moments

The Twelfth Of Never/I'm Afraid To Go Home

I Could Easily Fall (In Love With You) /I'm In

Love With You

This Was My Special Day/I'm Feeling Oh So Lonely

1 9 6 5

The Minute You're Gone/Just Another Guy

Angel/Razzle Dazzle

On My Word/Just A Little Bit Too Late The

Time In Between/Look Before You Love

Wind Me Up/The Night

1 9 6 6

Blue Turns To Grey/Somebody Loses

Visions/What Would I Do (For The Love Of A

Girl)

Time Drags By/The La La La Song

In The Country/Finders Keepers

1 9 6 7

It's All Over/ Why Wasn't I Born Rich?

I'll Come Running/I Get The Feelin'

The Day I Met Marie/Our Story Book All

My Love/Sweet Little Jesus Boy

1 9 6 8

Congratulations/High 'n' Dry

I'll Love Your Forever Today/Girl You'll Be

A Woman Soon

Marianne/Mr Nice

Don't Forget To Catch Me/What's More

(I Don't Need Her)

1 9 6 9

Good Times (Better Times)/Occasional Rain

Big Ship/She's Leaving You

Throw Down A Line (with Hank

Marvin)/Reflections

With The Eyes Of A Child/So Long

Albums

1 9 6 0

Me And My Shadows

1 9 6 1

Listen To Cliff

21 Today

The Young Ones

1 9 6 2

32 Minutes And 17 Seconds With Cliff Richard,

1 9 6 3

Summer Holiday

Cliff's Hit Album

When In Spain

1 9 6 4

Aladdin And His Wonderful Lamp

Wonderful Life!

1 9 6 5

Cliff Richard

More Hits By Cliff

When In Rome

Love Is Forever

1 9 6 6

Finders Keepers

Kinda Latin

1 9 6 7

Cinderella

Don't Stop Me Now

Good News

1 9 6 8

Cliff In Japan

Two A Penny

Established 1958

1 9 6 9

The Best Of Cliff

Sincerely Cliff Richard

Pantomimes

1 9 6 4

Aladdin And His Wonderful Lamp

1 9 6 6

Cinderella

Films

1 9 6 1

The Young Ones

1 9 6 2

Summer Holiday

1 9 6 4

Wonderful Life!

1 9 6 6

Finders Keepers

1 9 6 7

Two A Penny

The Seventies

High on personal growth,
relatively low on chart success –
the first part of the seventies gave
me time to get comfortable
with the way my career fitted
with my Christian life.
Then, unplanned but with
perfect timing, came the thrill
of an exciting new direction
in recording and a
number one single.

In the first half of 1970 I won a number of awards – the Song-writers Guild of Great Britain award for the Most Outstanding Service to Music in 1969, the Mr Valentine award from the *Disc And Music Echo*, Best-dressed Male Star and second British Male Singer, second British Vocal Personality, and Third Best World Singer according to a poll of readers of *The New Musical Express*. Coming third best in the world rather than first didn't bother me at all! I'd had my days at the very top and I was still around, happy to be near the top of the voting lists at the age of 30. With the Beatles about to disband – they finally split up in April 1970 – the mood of pop music was changing again, and I was no longer competing with top ten trends but rather, I hoped, becoming more established as an all-rounder in the entertainment business.

My first new ventures of the seventies were as a family entertainer on television and as a serious actor in a stage play. For my own 13-week television show, *It's Cliff Richard*, it was great to work with my dear friends Hank Marvin and Una Stubbs, while each week the prospective Eurovision song entries were previewed on the show and viewers chose *Knock Knock Who's There*, performed by Mary Hopkins, as the winner.

I have always been very conscious that my TV appearances go into millions of home and that there are thousands of young people watching whom I'd like to show that it is possible to be entertaining, sing good songs, have a chuckle, and have Christian values at the same time.

I'm happy to say that a number of viewers still tell the BBC that they welcome shows which they can look forward to watching together as a family, knowing beforehand that the show will contain nothing inappropriate or embarrassing for any generation of viewer.

For a long time I'd been hoping for an acting role in a non-musical production, and the opportunity came from the New Theatre in Bromley, Kent. I made my serious acting debut in *Five Finger Exercise* by Peter Schaeffer, later to gain a worldwide reputation as a playwright with *Equus*. My role was Clive Harrington, an artistic student who forms a deep friendship with his tutor, played by William Gaunt. I had my usual jitters about working with professional actors, although by now I did have

The awards rolled in during the early seventies and I hoped to become established as an all-round entertainer through new television and stage ventures.

considerable experience under my belt from films, television sketches and pantomimes, I knew that treading the boards in a real live theatre would demand acquiring and honing a new set of skills. And as usual, I needn't have worried because the cast were friendly and helpful throughout rehearsals. The only advice I could give them in return was on how to deal with eight curtain calls on the first night.

No one minded that some of my pop fans wanted to support me in my theatrical venture, too, because it meant the theatre was packed to the gills. I even got a good – well, might have been worse – review from the local *Kentish Times*, whose theatre critic said that my straight acting debut was: '...a triumph for Cliff's determination to make his way in the theatre.'

As the run of *Five Finger Exercise* came to the end, I released a single, *Goodbye Sam, Hello Samantha* (by Mitch Murray, Peter Callander and Geoff Stephens) with *You Never Can Tell* (by Hank Marvin) on the B-side. I always think of this as my fiftieth record. It reached number six in the charts – a significantly better result than my first single of the year *The Joy Of Living* – and was a popular number on my overseas tour in the summer of 1970.

Playing alongside actress Pamela Denton in Peter Schaeffer's Five Finger Exercise at the New Theatre in Bromley, Kent.

Another very interesting – and long – project was *The Cliff Richard Story* produced for BBC radio. Then during August I was back on television to star in a BBC special with Hank, Una, and star guest Aretha Franklin. Later in the year I appeared with the Settlers in three religious shows for the BBC, which began a pattern for my gospel shows which I have continued to undertake ever since – after performing gospel songs, I talk to the audience about Christianity and ending with a question and answer session with Bill Latham.

His Land, the film which I'd made on location in Israel in the early summer of 1969, was never released nationally to cinemas in Britain, but it was widely distributed for screenings in youth clubs and church halls in 1970 and, I hope, was entertaining as well as thought-provoking. Made by Worldwide Pictures, a division of the Billy Graham Organisation, the film took the form of a musical documentary on Israel, visiting the sites of many of the stories in the Bible.

My first LP of the seventies was *Cliff Live At The Talk Of The Town*, which was recorded live with Norrie Paramor conducting the Talk Of The Town Orchestra. The numbers included some old and new favourites – *Shout* and *Congratulations*; a few surprises, such as *A Taste Of Honey* and *Ain't Nothing But A House Party*; and a trio of songs by Hank entitled *Hank's Medley*. Later in the year, while I was again performing at The Talk Of The Town, my first religious album of the seventies was released. Much of the album was made up of my reading passages from the Bible, which I hoped would appeal to young people, teenagers and perhaps older listeners too.

To coincide with the screening of my television series, my album *Tracks 'N' Grooves* and the sound track LP of *His Land* were released in the same week. *Tracks 'N' Grooves* featured songs interpreted by four arranger-producers and achieved a good contrast to the previous LP. I included songs by Neil Diamond, Dick Holler, Charlie Rich, Neil Sedaka and

In a Wild West routine with Una Stubbs for my TV series It's Cliff Richard.

Carole Bayer Sager – a lively combination which I felt worked well. It was certainly a pleasure to record, as I got to sing many of my favourite tracks of the day. On the *His Land* album I sang alone on five tracks and chorus numbers included Ralph Carmichael adaptations of *Hava Nagila* and *Dry Bones*.

The first duet I recorded with Olivia Newton-John was *Don't Move Away*. She had sung backing vocals for me on tour, and this was a chance to give her the exposure she deserved. It became the B-side of *Sunny Honey Girl*, which was my first single of 1971, released at the beginning of another 13-week series for BBC television. Hank and Una were again resident guests and Hank presented his new group Marvin, Welch and Farrar, through whom I'd met Olivia. Peter Gormley was now managing Olivia too, and her first single *If Not For You* – a Bob Dylan song – was produced by Bruce and John Farrar and became a big hit in both the UK and in the States.

I established a close friendship with Olivia that added a special warmth to our duets on the series – I still love to sing with her – and I think viewers wished coupledom upon us. We both played a prank on a radio DJ by phoning him from a hotel room late one night, and, not surprisingly, that helped to fuel rumours.

I said, 'Hi this is Cliff Richard' and the DJ replied, 'Oh yes, and I'm Elvis Presley.'

Then Olivia rang up and said, 'Hello, this is Olivia Newton-John!'

The DJ used us as a running gag right through his programme, obviously thinking we were impostors.

Olivia and I had some great times together and I'm still very fond of her. I suppose it's because we never got involved that we can sustain a solid friendship and when we see each other, even though we hug each other like crazy for about ten minutes, there's no romance to revive. I feel totally comfortable with her and I would like to think she feels equally at ease with me. We had some great laughs making the sketches for the TV show in the seventies and since then have enjoyed singing

Left: April 1970 at Kingsway Hall in London, speaking and singing to a Christian audience. Above: With Olivia Newton-John, a long-standing friend who joined 'our gang' in the early seventies.

The first duet I recorded with Olivia was Don't Move Away. I still love to sing with her and we are still great friends.

together many times. Another TV appearance I made in the same year was as one of the narrators in a documentary describing a children's home in the Himalayan mountains where my aunt once worked. Also during the run of my TV series, I sang regularly on the radio in a religious series.

In April I released a single on an ecological theme – *Silvery Rain* by Hank Marvin. It didn't do too well in the charts, perhaps because it was a song before its time or because glitter rock was very much the craze then and remained so for a few years. However, this was a rewarding project because it concerned a theme close to our hearts – Hank and I had had many conversations about pesticides and pollution, and I thought this a good song.

From now on I didn't spend anywhere near as much time recording as I had done earlier in my career, but I was kept very busy with many other irons in the fire...

The New Theatre in Bromley had me back for a second time, complete with my first beard, to rehearse for a part in Graham Greene's 1958 play, *The Potting Shed*. I was very flattered, especially as the cast included established theatrical luminaries such as Patrick Barr and Kathleen Harrison. Our first night was made considerably more dramatic by a fire in the theatre only a couple of days before the opening night. The theatre was burned down and the production hastily moved to the Sadler's Wells Theatre in North London. Luckily for us, an Indian dance troupe had cancelled a week's booking, so we cut down on the scenery and wedged ourselves in. And I got my first West End stage première.

For this play the *Kentish Times* gave me a better review: 'In his performance as the obsessed James Callifer, Cliff Richard gives a nicely restrained performance that nevertheless has the undercurrent of poignancy and despairing drive.' I was happy with that.

In June Olivia, Hank, myself, Bruce Welch and John Farrar, got together again to join many stars including Petula Clark and Frankie Vaughan in a London Palladium tribute

Hank and I had many interesting – and sometimes heated – discussions on many topics over the years, and I enjoyed working with him on songs about themes close to our hearts.

I grew a rare beard for my part as James Callifer in Graham Greene's The Potting Shed.

concert to Dickie Valentine, the 50s singing idol who was a close relation of my longstanding road manager David Bryce.

Later in the summer, Olivia accompanied me to the festival of the Rose d'Or in France to receive an Ivor Novello Award for outstanding service to British music, then in August the gang – Olivia, Marvin, Welch, Farrar and I filmed *Getaway with Cliff* – a special programme for BBC. We also appeared in a three-week variety show at the Palladium which broke all records for pre-booked tickets, and not long afterwards we set off on a tour of Britain.

In the September of 1971 I was invited to perform at the opening rally of the Nationwide Festival Of Light at Westminster Central Hall in London. Christian groups were drawn into the pornography debate of the time and when I listened to the arguments, I found that Malcolm Muggeridge, Lord Longford and Mary Whitehouse made more sense than those who felt that exercising tolerance included banning rules against blasphemy and pornography. Since my early days as a pop star and more recently because of the reactions to my television shows, I remain convinced that people are influenced by everything they see and hear and that gratuitous violence and blasphemy have no place in mainstream entertainment.

My experience at the Festival Of Light rally dispelled any slight doubts I may have had as to which side I was on: it was my most unpleasant encounter with the Gay Liberation Movement who tried their best to disrupt the proceedings. I remember seeing a little old lady in the audience who had the misfortune to be sitting next to a burly chap who kept jumping up, shouting and cursing and shaking his fist. After about 20 minutes of his loud interruptions she walloped him round the head with her handbag.

The rally and the demonstration by Christians in Trafalgar Square and Hyde Park a few weeks later were memorable experiences for me – I saw proof that love can triumph over evil. A power radiated from that crowd that was almost tangible, an outgoing happiness and concern that stayed with me. I was jeered at and pelted with a few eggs by some people, but their efforts seemed paltry; the opposition couldn't deal with the lack of anger.

I do believe that protest has its place, but where do you draw the line? One could spend so much time complaining about what's wrong and achieve less than you would by getting on with what's right.

At this time I was over 30 and single and it seems that in our society a single person is deemed deserving of questions from total strangers about loneliness and/or sexual orientation that would be considered highly inappropriate for a married, or indeed many-times married person. I've now grown used to the question, 'So why have you never married, Cliff?' usually with built-in sub-plot about homosexuality.

The only answer I can give is that I've never met the right person. I do consider marriage as desirable but I do not see it as a prerequisite of a rewarding and worthwhile life. Each time I've fallen in love, I've thought, 'This is it, this is the one,' although it never worked out that way. If I had had a family I would certainly have been fully committed to it, which would have meant a completely different life, as my current commitments would have gone by the wayside. Perhaps for me – and many others – staying single is part of God's plan.

I've just had to get used to the fact that people who enjoy speculation and rumours need to look for something 'abnormal' about every person who is religious and single. Their intent is to be hurtful and they are. I won't pretend that all the sexual speculation isn't very painful for me – it's hurtful that in spite of all the things I do in life so much interest is aimed at the sexual side. I would say that although most people acknowledge the need to love and be loved, the majority could also imagine a fulfilling life outside marriage and sex, but it would be unfashionable to admit it.

On stage in the mid-seventies, behind Olivia and me you can just see (from left to right) Terry Britten, Alan Tarney and Trevor Spencer.

Wirral-based vicar Roy Barker handing over a cheque for Tear Fund to Bill Latham, who was Deputy Director of the charity in the seventies.

My next *Cliff Richard Show*, a television series, was in the first three months of 1972 and was minus Hank, who thought two series were enough, and Una who was expecting a baby. Dandy Nichols took Una's part (she played Una's mother in the hit TV comedy *Till Death Us Do Part*) and Olivia became a resident guest. The New Seekers had been selected to perform the UK entry for the 1972 Eurovision Song Contest and they played a song each week, from which viewers selected *Beg, Steal or Borrow* (and we won second place again).

In March I took part in a religious concert for Tear Fund at the New Century Hall in

Manchester. In April the *Sun* newspaper presented me with its Top Male Pop Personality award for the third year running.

1972 wasn't a busy year for my singles – *Flying Machine*, by George Kajanus, didn't exactly fly out of the record stores, then *Sing A Song of Freedom*, by Guy Fletcher and Doug Flett, reached number 13 but was banned in South Africa. I was disappointed when a great Nick Ingham production of a song called *Jesus* stayed in the charts for only three weeks, but this wasn't to be my period for hit singles and there was still time to record another later in the year when I came back from my tour of Europe and the Near and Far East. Live recordings were made in each country I visited on tour, to be released in the country of origin.

Living In Harmony, which I first performed on Lulu's television show, was my next single and my first recording of a song written by Alan Tarney and Trevor Spencer. Nick Ingham's arrangement used a country-style violin instead of the electronic sounds he'd used on *Jesus* and the result had a fresh edge. I sensed the beginning of a different sound. I also particularly enjoyed recording the B-side, *Empty Chairs*, written by Don McLean, author of *American Pie* and *Vincent*. *Living In Harmony* stayed in the charts for weeks while I was on a tour of Britain.

A musical/comedy/thriller film called *The Case* was a new venture for BBC2 television – very interesting but not very successful. I co-starred with Olivia Newton-John, comedian Tim Brooke-Taylor and two stars famous in Scandinavia (the film was part-financed by Scandinavian TV companies). Then came my last single of 1972, *A Brand New Song* – it was the first record I made without Norrie Paramor and my first not to make the top thirty. When Norrie retired from EMI and moved to Birmingham to conduct the Midland Light Orchestra, David MacKay took over on the production of my records – he was great to work with and I was mystified by the single's cold reception; I had really believed that *A Brand New Song* was hit material. However, it flopped well and truly so I knew I had to review the direction of my recordings, but I remained reluctant to emulate in any way the glam and glitter flavour of the charts at that time.

When *Congratulations* had just failed to win the Eurovision Song Contest for Britain I'd been bitterly disappointed, yet I was persuaded to have another go! At the start of 1973 I was invited to perform six songs on the *Cilla Black Show*. *Power To All Our Friends*, written by Guy Fletcher and Doug Flett was chosen as the British entry and it later sold more than a million copies to win me my sixth gold disc... but was placed third at the contest in Luxembourg in April.

My first film for seven years *Take Me High* was finished in November 1973 and opened nationally in December 1974. It must be included in any honest catalogue of my experiences, even though it was not a success. On paper the idea of *Take Me High* sparkled – the cast included Hugh Griffith, George Cole, Anthony Andrews and Richard Wattis in an all-singing, no-dancing musical for television. Filming took place in Birmingham and I played a young merchant banker involved in financial wrangles over the promotion of a new burger

I knew I had to review the direction of my recordings, but I remained reluctant to emulate in any way the glam and glitter flavour of the charts at that time.

joint with a gimmick – it was named a Brumburger! I sang eleven songs, every one related to the plot, which should give you an idea of the film's comedic challenges. In Thailand the film was released with the title *The Heavenly Sounds*, probably in the hope that Thais would enjoy the music even if the plot meant very little to them.

While making that film I was particularly pleased to get back to my new home in Weybridge, having moved from Totteridge I now attended Sunday evening services at Guildford Baptist Church as often as my work would allow. David Pawson, a noted Bible teacher, gave excellent sermons and didn't mind if I arrived at the last minute. Often there were no seats left and I'd plonk myself on the floor with other latecomers among a congregation of more than six hundred.

I was clearly perceived by some as out of sync with the mood of pop music at the time and when questioned by reporters I told the truth about rarely dating girls during the early 1970s, a fact which gained much more publicity than my Christian activities, and I spoke out against promiscuity.

My association with Tear Fund had taken on a new and more personal dimension after my visit to Bangladesh. When Bill Latham and George Hoffman invited me to join them on their visit to Tear Fund projects in 1973, the very least I could do was help make a soundstrip for presentations back in the UK, and I knew it would be a 'valuable experience'. Of course I had absolutely no concept of just how valuable.

Right: Meeting HRH the Duchess of Kent with my producer, great friend and mentor, Norrie Paramor. Below: Mamie Latham makes sure I eat my breakfast!

Cliff Richard

I went to Bangladesh en route back to the UK from Australia, where I had been performing at Sydney Opera House shortly after its official opening.

The Opera House is an inspiring architectural achievement and the atmosphere at its opening was one of high excitement, with Champagne flowing freely, sophisticated people, cultured conversation and moving music. Flying straight from all that into Dacca via Dum Dum Airport in Calcutta demanded a degree of emotional adjustment outside my experience. I found it very difficult, sometimes impossible, to cope.

We spent the first morning in one of the Bihari refugee camps and I have to admit that I must have washed my hands at least ten times. Whenever we stopped I walked in a daze to the communal tap or well; I didn't want to touch anything or, more to the point, anyone – everybody in the camps, even the babies and children, were covered in sores and scabs.

We were escorted by Liz Hutchison from Devon, one of the nurses whom Tear Fund was supporting. She said she hadn't taken us to the worst camps because we didn't have the Wellington boots necessary to walk through the sewage.

I wandered around in a state of shock, speechless. George understood my distress and quietly got on with taking the obligatory photographs. I was bending down next to one tiny child in front of the camera, horribly aware that I really did not want to touch the little mite, when someone accidentally stood on his fingers. The child screamed out and I instinctively grabbed hold of him. Forgetting all about his dirt and sores, it was the simple human reflex response to a child's cry of pain. The child stopped crying immediately and his frail form clung hard to my shoulder – in that moment teaching me more about Christian loving than words can say. I knew then that I had an enormous amount to learn about practical Christianity but at least I had made a start.

I have an enlargement of the snap that George took and I treasure it as one of my most meaningful possessions.

In the minibus on the way back to town I couldn't speak. It was a significantly more grown-up Cliff Richard that went back to the Intercontinental Hotel at the end of his first day in Bangladesh. I sat in a beautiful air-conditioned room with a glass of clear, iced water, feeling absolutely wretched and helpless in the face of such suffering.

On the evenings that followed we'd meet with the nurses in their home, sing a few songs and there would be lively discussion about the day's events, perhaps with some Bible verses that George had chosen to comment on.

I explained how utterly useless I felt. I'd seen people making an amazing contribution, a gruelling 24-hour commitment that was beyond my scope. Among such people I felt ashamed of my life of comfort. It seemed too easy, even cowardly, for me to go back to England, raise money from my Tear Fund concerts and enjoy every minute of it.

'What I've seen today makes me feel like giving up my life in England and staying here to try to help.' I said, struggling for words to express my emotions.

I love Australia – I've been visiting the country almost every year since my first Australian tour in 1961 and I was there for the opening of Sydney Opera House in 1973.

Cliff Richard   ✷ 107

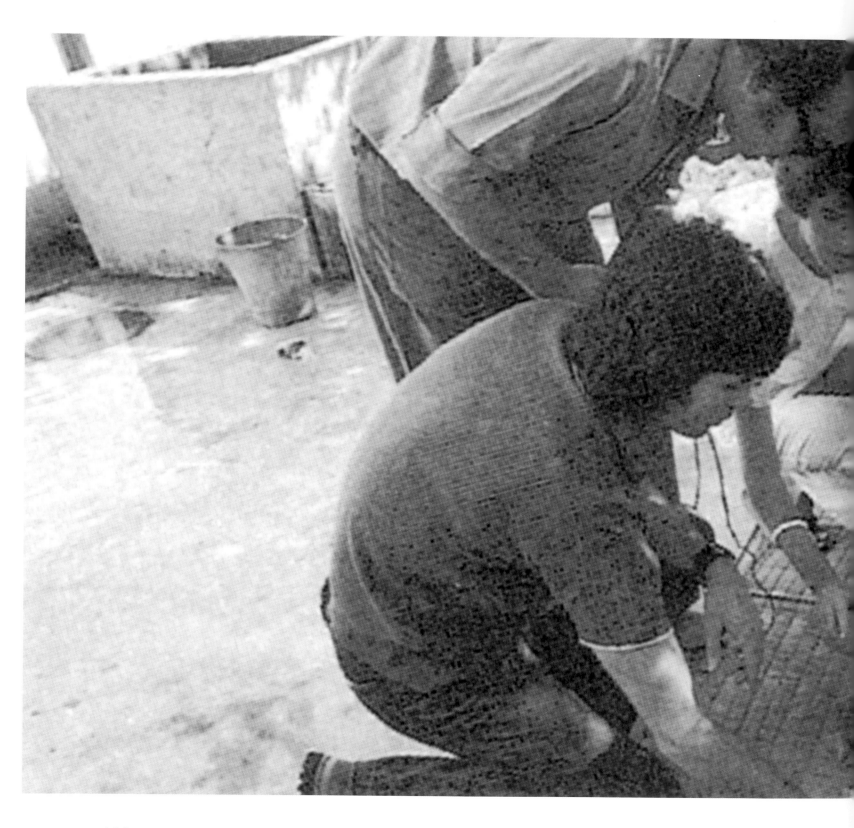

A Celebration

In 1973 I visited Bangladesh with Tear Fund. At the end of the first day I sat in an air-conditioned hotel room, feeling absolutely wretched and helpless in the face of such suffering.

Cliff

My backing group included some fine musicians who fortunately were to stay with me for years – Alan Tarney on bass, Trevor Spencer on drums, Kevin Peek and Terry Britten on guitar, and Cliff Hall on keyboards. I was very grateful to have such a talented team on board in the making of an album that was released for the financial benefit of the Tear Fund.

Liz Hutchison helped me out with a few simple truths: 'Can you give an injection or put someone on a drip..?' she asked me.

'No, I couldn't. I'd be horrified.'

'...Well, you'd be little use here...' she smiled. 'Go back home and raise money for us to do it. That's what you do and this is what we do. Without you and other Christians at home we couldn't be here. We need each other.'

On returning to England I reflected for a long time on the thoughts I had brought home with me from Bangladesh. Apart from a couple of television shows and a booking at the London Palladium, my only public appearance during the first part of 1974 was to receive an award from the Music Therapy Charity for outstanding services to the music industry.

The first of my two LPs of 1974 was *Help It Along* which had been recorded live in the September of the previous year. This was an album of mainly religious songs and featured some of my favourites of the time, such as *Jesus* and *Celestial Houses*, but we also included inspiring mainstream numbers such as *Amazing Grace*, *Day By Day* and James Taylor's *Fire And Rain*. My backing group included some fine musicians who fortunately were to stay with me for years – Alan Tarney on bass, Trevor Spencer on drums, Kevin Peek and Terry Britten on guitar, and Cliff Hall on keyboards. I was very grateful to have such a talented team on board in the making of an album that was released for the financial benefit of the Tear Fund.

A most enjoyable and unusual project of the second half of the year was landing the part of Bottom in Shakespeare's *A Midsummer Night's Dream*, staged by my old secondary school in Cheshunt. Rehearsals for the one-week run lasted six weeks and the cast was made up of old and current pupils. Of course, the production was the brainwave of Jay Norris, who was still teaching English there.

Another sign that my objectives and lifestyle were changing was that I released only one single – *You Keep Me (Hanging On)* – and this was my first year without a hit single. My second single was withdrawn after only a thousand copies had been pressed. It was entitled *Honky Tonk Angel*. When a girl in the audience at a Christian conference centre asked me, 'Why have you recorded a song about a prostitute?' her question shook me rigid.

'You're joking... aren't you?' I asked. 'I have sometimes rejected songs because their lyrics were unsuitable, anything offensive in these lyrics has completely passed me by!'

But the girl wasn't joking at all, so after the conference I got straight on the telephone to Peter Gormley to ask him to find out about any such connotations in the title. He spoke to some people in Los Angeles who confirmed that a honky tonk angel was not, as we'd imagined, an angelic-looking piano player in a bar, but at best a loose woman who frequented honky tonk bars.

I ordered the record to be stopped and had to explain to Russell Harty on his television show why I would not be performing my latest single. I was very concerned that

Cliff Richard

With the late George Thomas, then Speaker of the House of Commons. A gentle and much-loved man.

the early copies of the record would not become collectors' items so I contacted all the DJs who'd received one and took them back.

By the end of the year I felt ready to work on a new sound for a studio album. *The 31st Of February Street* was my first studio album since *Tracks 'N' Grooves* in 1970. I was backed by the same talented musicians as on *Help It Along*, with the addition of a steel guitarist, Gordon Huntley (a member of Matthews Southern Comfort who recorded *Woodstock* in 1970). The album included four songs which I wrote myself and a variety of moods. Listening to the tracks now, it seems clear that I was looking for a new type of sound but hadn't found it, so – as always – I wanted to try a new variety.

After the Shadows re-formed in 1974 we were invited to perform at a concert at the London Palladium the proceeds of which were for the widow of BBC producer Colin Charman. John Rostil had sadly died the previous year and his place was taken by John Farrar who, with Bruce Welch and Hank Marvin, produced my next single – *It's Only Me You've Left behind/You're the One*. Making a record can be very time-consuming when it's produced by three people, but this was a great trio to work in. I was very pleased with the result, if disappointed with public response. Sales of the single were were far fewer than *The Cliff Richard Story* – 6 LPs of earlier material which sold 250,000 boxed sets.

I didn't mind having nostalgic appeal, although perhaps a little less a little later would have been preferable! However, I remained optimistic about the future of my career; I knew that in so many ways my life was in transition. I had never been busier or more fulfilled and if the hits were meant to be, they would come along again. In fact my 'comeback' happened suddenly – with my first single of 1975, followed by an exciting new direction with an LP and my return to the American charts.

Peter Gormley and I were looking for a producer who could come up with the most good songs with a new sound, and it was Bruce Welch who rose to the challenge and hit on the right balance of songs for my next album – *I'm Nearly Famous*.

The first two songs Bruce suggested were written by Terry Britten – *Devil Woman* and *I Wish You'd Change Your Mind*. Michael Denne and Ken Gold provided two great tracks, then we selected four songs – including the title track – by two relatively new young songwriters, Michael Allison and Peter Sills. And we also chose songs from American songwriters including Mickey Newbury and David Pomeranz. We were about halfway through the recording sessions when I realised that something new and different was happening. *Devil Woman* had been hanging around my music room for 18 months or more, but as I was interpreting the song I sensed a new freedom and sense of adventure, and when we played it back Tony Clark the engineer shouted 'America! This will be a smash in America!'

With *Can't Ask For Anything More*, for example, I dared to sing falsetto – something I'd only done on stage before.

I sensed the magic of *Miss You Nights* the first time I heard it. Produced by Bruce

Cliff Richard   ★ 113

Welch, with orchestral arrangement by Andrew Powell and vocal arrangement by Tony Rivers, the single had a dramatic sound. It was released in February 1976, before *Devil Woman* because there was a risk of the latter being confused with the ELO's *Evil Woman* which had entered the charts in January. *Miss You Nights* only reached number 15 in the charts but it has remained a favourite. Then came *Devil Woman*, released as a single in April, which took the charts by storm – when the record was released as a single in April 1976 it went to number nine in Britain and number six in the United States, while the *I'm Nearly Famous* album quickly rose to number five in the album charts.

Terry Britten heard a DJ play the first few bars on radio and ask people to phone in and guess who was about to sing on the record. Everyone was getting it wrong before they heard the track and there seemed to be real excitement at the news that I could make a record like this one.

When I did *Devil Woman* on *Top Of The Pops* six months later, someone heard a little boy turn to his father when he saw me singing and say, 'Is it him singing? I thought it was some black bloke!'

I'm Nearly Famous was my first entry in the UK album charts for years and within months of its release it spawned at least three hit singles in dozens of countries all round the world.

The worldwide reaction was phenomenal. I saw the promotional *I'm Nearly Famous* T-shirts at concerts in many countries for years after, and what a hoot to see photographs of no less than Elizabeth Taylor and Elton John sporting *I'm Nearly Famous* badges at a reception in far-away Philadelphia!

There's no doubt that it was Elton's firey enthusiasm, together with remarkable professionalism and sheer hard work from people at his Rocket Records, that put *Miss You Nights* and *Devil Woman* on the road to success in the States. I loved getting weekly phone calls from Los Angeles with reports on the progress of *Devil Woman* as it moved up the charts.

I also have to thank Elton's mother for taking her son to the Palladium, because according to her he's been a fan of mine ever since he saw me in pantomime there when he was 13.

One music paper described 1976 as 'the year of the Cliff Richard renaissance'. My chart success was rekindled and I'd

Elton John's Rocket Records released Devil Woman in 1976 and gave me my first American top ten hit, while the album I'm Nearly Famous was my first entry in the US album charts for years.

Kenny Everett and I discussing an exhibition of photographs. I appreciated Kenny's contribution to the television programme Why Should the Devil Have All the Good Music? *some years later, when he expressed some thoughtful views about my faith.*

broken into the American market with *Devil Woman*. Through working with different producers I had become much more interested in the whole recording process and now involved myself in the early stages of creating an album, talking to writers and so helping choose musical arrangements, then the mixing and even the design of the album sleeve. In the past, although I'd always enjoyed recording, it was often a matter of turning up at the studio and taking instructions for the day ahead, then taking an hour or two at the most to lay down each song. That changed completely from the *I'm Nearly Famous* album onwards.

Signing with Elton John's label, Rocket Records, in America had attracted some negative publicity in this country, while in America it seemed to act as a timely reminder of who I was and how successful I had been on other continents.

In Russia my records were now sold officially, rather than on the black market, through the Melodia label. I received an invitation to perform there from the official State Entertainments Department – Gosconcerts – which must have decided that my music was 'culturally acceptable' for Russian youth. And so I became the first Western pop-rock artist to be declared blemish-free, but I have to admit that I was a little wary of visiting Russia and postponed the tour once.

Before I went there my idea of Russia was perhaps over-coloured by James Bond movies. What really surprised me was that when we performed in Moscow and Leningrad for three weeks in 1976 the Russians raised no objections to my gospel numbers. I'd heard all about censorship and thought I might run into deep water with some of my songs. But I sang *When I Survey The Wondrous Cross* and no one turned a hair.

And I was completely wrong to anticipate a rather cool and serious reception and to imagine that middle-aged officials would outnumber the teenagers.

Every one of the 20 concerts we gave was sold out weeks before we arrived. On the first night in Leningrad we had to open the orchestra pit to stop enthusiastic young Russians leaping on stage to give everyone a bear hug. And every performance was an exhilarating experience for me – each night, as the audience warmed up, crowds of people would rush down to the barriers in front of the stage, singing, clapping to the rhythm and making

Above: A signing session for my Every Face Tells a Story album in a London department store. Right: With the Shadows at the Café Royal in 1977 collecting a Music Therapy Charity award for 'outstanding services to the music industry'.

peace signs. I was surprised to find that Moscow Baptist Church squeezed in a huge congregation for not one but three Sunday services! After a late Saturday night, I managed to get to church in time for a ten o'clock service on the Sunday morning and was ushered towards a special pew kept for visitors.

As a fabulous choir finished singing the anthem, my heart sank when I saw the choirmaster making a beeline for me. Before the service he'd asked if I'd sing something but I'd explained that I'd rather not because nothing melodious seems to emerge from my throat in the mornings.

'I just wondered if you had changed your mind about singing?' he whispered loudly in English. I couldn't refuse now and from a packed balcony in Moscow Baptist Church I sang in a rather husky voice, but for me never more emotional, 'When I survey the wondrous cross on which the Prince of Glory died, my richest gain I count but loss, and pour contempt on all my pride'.

Everyone in the church stood up, every member of the congregation silent and still, and our understanding of each other was perfect. Different languages, cultures and lifestyles didn't matter. We were one family in Jesus.

There were those who criticised my Russian tour, as they did my visits to South Africa, saying that by working in a country I condone its policies. I do not share that opinion. I'm still enough of an idealist to hope that a little bridge of communication may have been set up on many occasions which wouldn't have happened if I'd stayed at home.

Following on from the success of *I'm Nearly Famous*, Bruce began producing another album with me at the end of 1976, which was released in 1977 – *Every Face Tells A Story* featured many of the same writers who had contributed to *I'm Nearly Famous*. Two songs from this album were released as singles whose B-sides were not on the album; they were written by me – *No One Waits* and *Nothing Left To Say* were the respective B-sides of *Hey Mr. Dream Maker* and *My Kinda Life*.

Fortunately I was able to work with Bruce and the same musicians for a new religious album, *Small Corners*, released around the same time as a double album, *40 Golden Greats*. Forty tracks meant we had to omit about thirty hits, so we were happy to know we'd chosen a winning selection when the LP topped the album charts for a week in October 1977.

Small Corners carried some fantastic tracks in my mind, particularly those by the rock 'n' roll evangelist, American Larry Norman – *Why Should The Devil Have All The Good Music*, *Up In Canada* and *I Wish We'd All Been Ready*.

In May 1977 I took part in a successful youth rally at Windsor Great Park during the

I'm still enough of an idealist to hope that my singing in a foreign country may set up a small bridge of communication that would not exist if I stayed at home.

Collecting the Music Week award, presented to me and the Shadows in celebration of 21 years as major British recording artists.

Queen's Silver Jubilee celebrations, and in October I was honoured with two surprise awards – Best British Male Solo Artist from the British Phonographic Institute and the Gold Badge Award from the Songwriters' Guild Of Great Britain.

What an amazing surprise to have a hit at the end of the 1970s which topped the success of *Congratulations*, *The Young Ones* and *Living Doll*! *We Don't Talk Any More*, from my *Rock 'n' Roll Juvenile* album and written by Alan Tarney, sold more than five million copies and reached the Top 20 in the American charts, marking the beginning of a period of steady American chart success. And in Britain it held the number one spot for four weeks. I'd just arrived back from holiday in Portugal when the record got to number one, and after enjoying my usual long and loud welcome from my dogs Kelly and Emma, I sat down to deal with a non-stop string of telegrams and telephone calls. Time after time I was asked, 'How does it feel to be number one again after all these years?'

And time after time I did not play it cool: 'It feels amazing, fantastic, absolutely wonderful..!'

I'd just arrived back from holiday when We Don't Talk Anymore reached number one – I completely lost my cool!

Singles

1 9 7 0

The Joy Of Living (with Hank Marvin)/*Leave My Woman Alone/Boogatoo* (Hank Marvin)

Goodby Sam, Hello Samantha/You Can Never Tell

I Ain't Got Time Anymore/Monday Comes Too Soon

1 9 7 1

Sunny Honey Girl/Don't Move Away (with Olivia Newton-John)/*I Was Only Fooling Myself*

Silvery Rain/Annabella Umbrella/Time Flies

Flying Machine/Pigeon

Sing A Song Of Freedom/A Thousand Conversations

1 9 7 2

Jesus/Mr Cloud

Living In Harmony/Empty Chairs

A Brand New Song/ The Old Accordion

1 9 7 3

Power To All Our Friends/Come Back Billie Jo

Help It Along/Tomorrow Rising

The Days Of Love/Ashes To Ashes

Take Me High/Celestial Houses

1 9 7 5

(You Keep Me) Hangin' On/Love Is Here

It's Only Me You've Left Behind/You're The One

Honky Tonk Angel (Wouldn't You Know It)/Got Myself A Girl

1 9 7 6

Miss You Nights/Love Enough

Devil Woman/Love On (Shine On)

I Can't Ask For Anything More Than You/Junior Cowboy

Hey Mr Dream Maker/ No One Waits

1 9 7 7

My Kinda Life/Nothing Left For Me To Say

When Two Worlds Drift Apart/That's Why I Love You

1 9 7 8

Yes! He Lives/Good On The Sally Army Please

Remember Me/Please Don't Tease

Can't Take The Hurt Anymore/Needing A Friend

1 9 7 9

Green Light/Imagine Love

We Don't Talk Anymore/Count Me Out

Hot Shot/Walking In The Light

Albums

1 9 7 0

Cliff Live At Talk Of The Town

About That Man

His Land

Tracks And Grooves

1 9 7 2

The Best Of Cliff Volume Two

1 9 7 3

Take Me High

1 9 7 4

Help It Along

The 31st Of February Street

1 9 7 6

I'm Nearly Famous

1 9 7 7

Every Face Tells A Story

40 Golden Greats

1 9 7 8

Small Corners

Green Light

1 9 7 9

Thank You Very Much

Rock And Roll Juvenile

Theatre

1970
Five Finger Exercise by Peter Schaeffer,
Bromley New Theatre

1971
The Potting Shed by Graham Greene,
Sadler's Wells Theatre

1974
A Midsummer Night's Dream
by WIlliam Shakespeare,
Riversmead School, Cheshunt

Film

1970
His Land, Worldwide Pictures

1973
Take Me High, Anglo EMI Films

Cliff Richard

The Eighties

A successful London concert season, three singles in the American charts at the same time, a wonderful tour of South Africa, some great surprises in poll awards and a great shock at being awarded the OBE! All that - as well a truly surprising fortieth birthday party - happened in 1980; my life didn't begin at 40 but the new decade promised to be quite lively...

Cliff

I'd been voted top male vocalist before, but never by under-16s — and in my fortieth year!

Cliff

When I heard my name was on the New Year Honours list of 1980 it didn't come as a complete surprise. In the previous autumn I'd received a letter with an impressive heading informing me, in the traditional wording, that there was a possibility of my being considered for an honours award and would I indicate whether, in principle, I was prepared to accept.

My initial reaction was to write to decline in as courteous a manner as possible, but fortunately I slept on my decision and the following day refocused my thoughts. When it was all over I felt a little guilty for having considered declining the honour even for a minute.

I must admit that my first reaction was defensive. I could imagine cynical people only too ready to dismiss my involvement with Christians as a means of ingratiating myself with the Establishment. I could almost hear the familiar critical tones of their voices. It would be easier to turn it down, no one would ever know and there would be no fuss or possibility of criticism from any quarter.

After more thought I realised I was letting the gripers tinge my judgment. Rather than be concerned about cynics I should accept and appreciate an honour at face value and be more concerned about the people who would be pleased and encouraged by my receiving it. The award was not just for me but for what – and Whom – I stood.

My fans and friends gave me a sense that I was receiving the OBE as much for them as for me.

Soon after the New Year announcement, jokes flew around about the Oldest British Entertainer but I still couldn't quite believe that any kind of OBE might actually apply to me.

The early 1980s were notable years for awards in a completely different category from the OBE but nonetheless very important to me. I gained a whole bundle of new awards from the entertainment industry.

The biggest surprise was an award voted for by children. Listeners to Noel Edmond's *Swap Shop* on Saturday morning TV voted me the country's top male vocalist. I'd been voted top male vocalist before, but never by under-16s – and in my fortieth year! I think my nearest rival in the poll was Gary Numan. In the National Rock and Pop Awards organised by Radio 1, *Nationwide* and the *Daily Mirror* I was named Best Family Entertainer. Outstanding Music Personality of the Year came 12 months later from *Daily Mirror* readers and was presented to me by Una Stubbs at the Café Royal. Then in May 1981 I was voted Top Pop Star in the *Sunday Telegraph* readers' poll. I enjoy the thought of the readers of two such different newspapers all enjoying listening to my music, while the editors strive to appeal to such opposite sets of tastes and styles.

Also in May 1981 the *TV Times* readers voted me Most Exciting Male Singer on television – not bad for a fortysomething.

To add to those successes were a sell-out UK gospel tour and a three-week show at

My mother came with me to
Buckingham Palace when I was
presented with my OBE. It was
fantastic to be able to share
that moment with her.

Cliff

the Apollo Victoria in London, which sold out through postal bookings even before the box office had opened. And another memorable achievement was the televising of our gospel concert in Chichester, in my opinion the most enjoyable and best television I've ever done. Artists and musicians put in so much hard work, time and creativity to perfecting a certain sound in a recording studio, and it can be very disheartening when television produces a show with sound that is very flat in comparison to the real thing. In Chichester there was no risk of that, because Southern TV (now sadly disenfranchised) gave us plenty of studio time to overdub and remix after the recording.

In February 1980 I performed at a special concert in tribute to Norrie Paramor at the Fairfield Hall in Croydon, attended by the Duchess of Kent. With backing from the Ron Goodwin Orchestra and Tony Rivers, John Perry and Stu Calver, I sang six songs with particularly strong associations with Norrie – *Bachelor Boy*, *Constantly*, *The Day I Met Marie*, *Congratulations*, *The Young Ones*, and *Summer Holiday*. I was glad to have an opportunity of singing my goodbye to Norrie: I had missed him enormously in the months since his death and still think of him often, realising more and more as I look back over the years and forward to new plans and projects what an enormously positive influence he had on my career.

Also In February my single *Carrie* was released and was to reach number four in the UK charts and enter the American Top 40. In February and March of 1980, I had a busy and very enjoyable tour of South Africa – Durban, Port Elizabeth, Cape Town and Johannesburg and, back in England, work began in the new Riverside studios with with Alan Tarney and Trevor Spencer on recordings for a new album.

Without Norrie there was a gap which could not be filled in a short space of time and a great sadness about recording without him around. While Peter Gormley's idea of giving Bruce Welch both the job of choosing and producing new material had worked extremely well on *I'm Nearly Famous*, *Every Face Tells A Story* and *Green Light*, it would be a difficult and comprehensive role for Alan Tarney to follow in the production of my next album, entitled *I'm No Hero*.

The track chosen for pre-release as a single was *Dreamin'* and I had a very good feeling about the choice. I also had a certain date before that single release fixed in my mind: I looked forward with excitement tinged with a little terror to July 23, the day I received my OBE at Buckingham Palace.

An excellent suit had been hanging in my wardrobe for years just waiting for the right formal occasion – and the investiture ceremony at Buckingham Palace was surely it, or so I thought. Luckily I discovered just in time from an etiquette-know-all friend that wearing that particular suit would have been a terrible gaffe – it was an evening suit and not suitable for a morning-dress occasion. So I hastily put the tails back into mothballs and got out a plain dark suit, red silk tie and a pair of red and bouncy Italian shoes which I thought would make a good match for the Palace carpet.

It was fantastic to be able to share the moment with my mother, who came with me to Buckingham Palace. She had supported me in all my dreams and schemes but the OBE came as a complete surprise and the event was even more moving than either of us had anticipated.

Earlier in the day I had spoken calmly with Mike Read on Radio One about how thrilled and honoured I felt, but when the time of the ceremony arrived my heart seemed to be thumping loud in my ears and I could hardly speak. I was told where, how and when to stand up, and discovered that the knighthoods were being 'done' first so the rest of us about-to-be OBEs had to wait in the wings. I had been looking forward to seeing some of that time-honoured dubbing with the sword, but instead I was able to chat with all kinds of interesting people while we were waiting.

As we formed a queue to receive our honours, I looked over my shoulder to see whether I could spot my mother sitting at the other end of the hall. She was wearing a

Right: Daily Mirror readers have chosen me for many awards over the years. As the eighties began, the Daily Mirror presented me with the Nationwide Golden Award for Best Family Entertainer.

Cliff Richard ✳ 131

Reaching the age of forty is regarded as some kind of landmark, but I felt no different and managed to pack in a lot of celebrating.

bright pink hat, so I thought I'd be able to spot her quite quickly, but as my eyes scanned the seated crowd, dozens and dozens of bright pink hats seemed to be bobbing everywhere like a field of cerise flowers. Mum must have chosen the 'in' colour for investitures that season!

I approached the Queen on the dais. Did I imagine it or was there a momentary look of relief on her face? Perhaps because she recognised me and wouldn't have to ask me what I did? I can't recall the exact words, but I remember the Queen told me that she was particularly delighted to give me the award as I had 'been around for rather a long time!'.

The formal atmosphere suddenly lifted as I left the dais and the band struck up *Congratulations*.

Outside the Palace there was a party atmosphere. A coachload of fans had travelled from the Midlands and some from even further afield. And I knew that somewhere among the crowds jammed outside the palace gates were my sisters and friends. After the slight tension before the ceremony and the excitement of the crowds, it was good to arrive at the peaceful Arts Centre at Waterloo where we held a small private lunch to celebrate.

Another out-of-the-blue achievement of that summer, and something I'd almost given up hoping for, was the American success of *Dreamin'*. The single climbed the charts on both sides of the Atlantic and reached both Top Tens in the same month. The song was written by Alan Tarney and Leo Sayer, and I was also particularly proud of the B-side of that single, an updated version of *Dynamite* which I'd first released as the B-side to *Travellin' Light* some 21 years earlier!

We Don't Talk Anymore had perhaps paved the way for a successful year in the American charts. When it reached the Top 20 of the US Hot 100 in 1979 it was my first Stateside hit for three years and for the first time in 20 years the international branch of EMI showed real interest in releasing my records in America. That hit seemed to trigger a following for my music in the States which led to three of my singles making the Hot 100 in 1980 and another four in 1981.

★

I'd almost given up hope of chart success in the States, but it came out of the blue with Dreamin'

'How does it feel to be forty?' I must have been asked that question a hundred times around the time of my fortieth birthday, October 14,1980.

'Fine thanks,' I'd reply. 'Much the same as yesterday and no different from my thirtieth birthday actually.'

I'm not sure why the age of 40 is supposed to be such a landmark, but I got more phone calls, mail, telegrams and press attention on that day than on any other birthday before. And I managed to pack in a lot of celebrating.

On the day of my birthday I was in concert at the Apollo in London and it seemed as if every single person in the audience had come with a card or flowers to bring to the

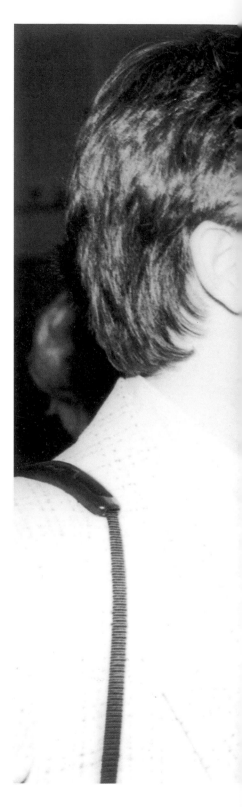

Paul McCartney and I have met on only a few occasions but we share a little piece of history as 'veterans' of the entertainment industry – and I think there's still a jokey competitiveness there!

stage. Throughout the two hours of the concert there was a constant stream of people walking up to the stage and putting flowers, cards and parcels around my feet. And every now and then a verse of *Happy Birthday* would be taken up very loudly by the whole audience.

The numbers I sang included *Move It, Carrie, Miss You Nights, Give A Little Bit More, Everyman, The Young Ones, Living Doll* and *A Little In Love*. There were so many surprises that I was expecting something to happen after – or during – every song. One of my guitarists transformed a moody instrumental section in one number into a funky version of *Happy Birthday*, which upstaged me completely. As I came to the end of another song Colin and Bob, sound and lighting engineers, arrived on stage carrying a humungous birthday cake and told me not to worry about the lighting controls.

I could barely squeeze into my dressing room for flowers, cards and presents. And one large parcel in the middle of the room had wooden feet sticking out at the bottom which I thought I recognised. Everyone except me seemed to be in the know about this one and people were urging me to open it.

I'd become hooked on an electronic asteroids game at the recording studio where Alan Tarney and I had worked together and I'd asked for the same game to be installed in my dressing room at the Apollo – if you're going to spend six hours a day in a little box you need a diversion. I was delighted at the delivery of a fine item of furniture housing the said asteroid game and had spent many happy hours with it blasting and bleeping away to try and improve my score.

When the wraps came off my chunky fortieth birthday present there was an identical asteroids machine, bearing an engraved plate which read 'To Cliff, 40 years and three sell-out weeks.' It was a present from Eddie Jarrett, my agent and friend for many years, and Paul Gregg, the theatre owner.

I'd been thoroughly hoodwinked into looking forward to a quiet family dinner at the Waterloo Arts Centre after all the excitement at the theatre, but I should have known better. I was gently propelled through the door of a room that was packed to the gills with the beaming faces of my closest friends from all over the country, from church, from the office, and of course my

Cliff Richard   ☀ 135

family, all people I love and respect deeply. Most of them had a prompt nine o'clock start for work next morning, but the party went on until four.

A lot of planning and ingenuity went into that party – it was a complete surprise and meant a great deal to me, because it brought into perspective all the other successes of the year. To have such a wonderful group of friends like that, from many different walks of life and nearly all Christians, is especially important for me in keeping me off any lonely showbiz pedestal and in touch with the things that really matter in life.

A little musical surprise involving a great friend was the opportunity to record a song with Olivia Newton-John. The *Xanadu* film project took off for Olivia, who got to dance with Gene Kelly. The film's musical score was mostly composed by Jeff Lynne of the Electric Light Orchestra and John Farrer included a string of hits. For one of the tracks for the film I recorded a duet, *Suddenly*, with Olivia and it was released as a single. Following her appearance in the smash-hit film *Grease*, Olivia had become popular all over the world and in *Xanadu* she was seen on screen singing many other great songs, while *Suddenly* was only heard as part of the sound track. Nevertheless our duet made the Top Twenty on both sides of the Atlantic and stayed in the British charts for seven weeks.

Throughout the eighties I was flattered to receive many requests from other artists wanting to record duets. Andrew Lloyd-Webber asked me to record *All I Ask Of You*, from *Phantom Of The Opera*, with Sarah Brightman. Dave Clark added my vocal to a track produced by Stevie Wonder for the musical *Time*, A&M records suggested a duet with Janet Jackson, and Elton John invited me to join him singing *Slow Rivers*.

Again, Americans were buying my records even though I'd done relatively little to promote them in their terms. Another track from my *I'm No Hero* album, *A Little In Love*, peaked at number 11 in the American charts at the end of 1980 and reached number 15 in the British charts at the beginning of 1981.

Meeting Mother Teresa was a wonderful experience. What I remember most is the simplicity of her grace – her simple surroundings, simple manner, simple words and simple wisdom, which were the foundations of her magnificent work.

I'd had a string of chart hits in America without really trying and I now felt determined to do a no-holds-barred concert tour without worrying too much about profit margins – other people could do that. I wanted to play to some of those people in the States who had been buying my singles and getting them into their charts.

It's a bit like people say about climbing Everest, it's there and it's big, so why not revisit America? I knew it would be a gruelling tour and a great challenge but the changing tastes and different states of America make irresistible territory for a British artist because it's vast and because it's completely different from touring Europe or, say, a concert series in Japan.

We decided against putting a few all-American famous names alongside mine to bring in the audiences – my name alone would have to do that, so it was a big risk.

The tour began on a sour note when one of our trucks was stolen while we were rehearsing in Hollywood. It had about £40,000's worth of musical instruments and sound equipment inside but there was no time to dither about: to prepare for a seven-week coast-to-coast tour the whole lot simply had to be replaced as quickly as possible.

The tour started in Seattle on March 3 and ended on April 18 at the Santa Monica Civic Auditorium in Los Angeles. We appeared in more than 30 theatres and, in between almost nightly concerts, I did the round of radio interviews, chat shows and phone-ins. I knew that, despite my increased record sales in the States, the majority of people you stopped on a city street would never have heard of me. I also knew that things would probably stay that way unless I spent some time living in America – which I have no desire to do (I've aways felt that four months away from home was long enough for me). The New York and Los Angeles concerts were sell-outs and I received a particularly warm welcome at most of the concerts in Canada.

A couple of weeks after I'd returned from the States I starred in a special one-off concert at the Hammersmith Odeon in London on May 1. The concert was filmed and footage from it used as part of the opening programme in a television series shown on BBC at the end of the year.

I was happy to take part in the series. Although I was surprised that anyone wanted to make four different programmes about me, I also knew that this meant that a significant amount of time would be dedicated to the importance of religion in my life and the producer, Norman Stone, would be giving me an important opportunity to speak about my faith to a huge television audience. Film of the concert on my fortieth birthday was included and also some clips taken at my surprise party afterwards, in which I looked completely nonplussed and glassy-eyed when I walked into that room full of friends at the Christian Arts Group Centre in Waterloo.

It's a bit like people say about climbing Everest, it's there and it's big, so why not revisit America? I knew it would be a gruelling tour and a great challenge but the changing tastes and different states of America make irresistible territory for a British artist...

This photograph was taken around the time of the release of Wired for Sound – I had good reason to look pleased, because the album became my best seller since I'm Nearly Famous.

Cliff Richard

Because Norman cleverly mixed together old and new footage and interviewed many people whom I'd known and worked with as early as 1958, the programme was very enjoyable for me. Bruce and Tito both took part. Adam Faith spoke about the atmosphere in the 2i's; John Foster and Ian Samwell reminded me of my very first performances and the passion we all shared for rock 'n' roll. And Marty Wilde gave us all a fine trip back in time by taking the cameraman around the Hackney Empire where *Oh Boy!* was filmed.

The second programme in the BBC's *Cliff* series was subtitled *Why Should The Devil Have All The Good Music?*, the Larry Norman song which opened the show. It offered me the opportunity to focus on the religious side of my work, to pay tribute to other religious artists whom I admire and to try to explain to fans what exciting and uplifting experiences Christianity brings into my life.

To have such famous personalities express their views about faith – including Kenny Everett, Olivia Newton-John, Dave Lee Travis, Mike Read and Adam Faith – gave support to my conviction that my Christianity is widely acknowledged and accepted by friends and fans. Phil Everly agreed to appear and I thoroughly enjoyed performing with him when we sang *All I Have To Do Is Dream* and *When WIll I Be Loved* together.

Phil said such fantastic things about me that I wasn't at all surprised when Norman Stone, to redress the balance a bit, decided to find somebody willing to criticise me at some length. Neil Spencer was editor of the *New Musical Express* and mad about reggae music. He claimed that I had been disloyal to my fans in the early sixties because I had 'abandoned' rock 'n' roll. My only response was that I knew of very few rock stars who were around in the sixties who still sing rock 'n' roll to large audiences as often as I do.

The television series touched me with mixed emotions, but mostly very happy memories came flooding back and it seemed fitting that my most recent album that had been prepared for release that summer should have a sentimental flavour. It was a compilation album of all the favourite love songs I'd ever recorded and it became a num-

Shakin' Stevens, Alvin Stardust and me, all very happy to acknowledge the influence of Elvis Presley!

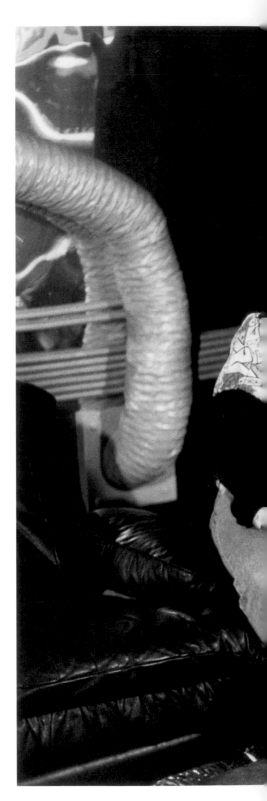

Cliff Richard 141

ber-one best-selling LP for five weeks (my fifth number one album). *Love Songs* spent a total of 43 weeks in the charts, so it was still very popular when the television series was screened in the run-up to Christmas. But anyone who thought I'd permanently deserted rock 'n' roll for smooth and smoochy love songs was surely forced to reconsider when my next album was released – *Wired For Sound*.

The title track, *Wired For Sound*, is a great Tarney track, with lyrics by B A Robertson. No sooner had I first heard the song than I had a strong feeling that it would be a big hit and the recording sessions only served to make me enjoy the song even more. When it was released as a single (only a couple of weeks after *Love Songs* had dropped out of the Number One position in the LP charts) it went into the charts at number five, moved to number four the following week and then stayed in the charts for the rest of the year.

Alan Tarney was producer of the *Wired For Sound* recording sessions which took place at the Gallery Studios, with additional accompaniments from musicians including Trevor Spencer and Graham Jarvis on drums, and John Clarke and Nick Glennie-Smith on guitar and keyboards.

A contrasting hit single came with *Daddy's Home*, a song which had been a 1961 hit in America for Shep and the Limelights and which I'd been recorded singing for the BBC television series. The live recording was added to the *Wired For Sound* album. Released as a single with another live track, *Shakin' All Over*, on the B-side it became my biggest hit of the year, reaching

Standing on the same podium as Billy Graham gave me a different kind of stage fright. I needed faith in myself to find the right words.

Cliff Richard   ✳ 143

Right: Sue Barker and I at a London theatre in June 1982. Sue insisted that I was too old to become proficient at tennis, but I've tried and it's been great fun developing the Tennis Trails.

number two in the singles charts.

The reception given to my records in America remained a surprise, as *Wired For Sound* made little impact in comparison with its reception in the UK – at the beginning of 1981 *Dreamin'* and *A Little In Love* had made the Hot 100, followed by *Give A Little Bit More*, a track from *I'm No Hero* which was not considered appropriate for release as a single in the UK.

My 1981 Album *Now You See Me, Now You Don't* was an interesting venture in that I produced it myself in co-operation with a little known American session musician, Craig Pruess. He had previously headed a band called Visitor 2035 and I'd met him when he was working on recording sessions playing keyboard and synthesiser. We planned a gospel album, and it was the first time I described my Christian music as Rockspel.

I knew people would say the album was neither one thing nor the other, but it was very satisfying for me not to have to divide my musical tastes in two and to produce an album simply offering music that I enjoyed. One track which happily mixed the ancient and modern was *Little Town*, a treatment of the carol *O Little Town Of Bethlehem*, which became a Top 10 hit and meant that I was able to appear on *Top Of The Pops* for Christmas 1982.

It was around this time that I began a friendship with Sue Barker, a fellow Christian who happened to be one of the world's most famous female tennis players. It was impossible to spend five minutes with Sue without becoming fascinated by tennis. I'd always been interested in playing tennis, although not on a regular basis, but after meeting Sue I became more seriously involved – some of my holiday companions might say obsessed – with the game. Sue insisted that, taking up the sport in my forties, I had no hope of becoming proficient, but that's just the kind of challenge I enjoy. The best compliment I've had is from the tennis commentator Warren Jacques who once said that had I started playing as a child I might have been good enough to sneak in to a minor county team. The main point is that I enjoy tennis and it keeps me in shape.

The great thing that came out of my 'obsession' is the pro-celebrity Tennis Tournaments. They help fund the Tennis Trails, sponsoring professional coaching in schools to help develop and nurture tennis skills among children while serving up some useful health education on the side.

My next album, *Dressed For The Occasion*, was recorded at the Albert Hall, where for the first time I was accompanied by the London Philharmonic Orchestra. Then in 1983 we made an album entitled *Silver*. This album was accompanied by the *Rock 'n' roll Silver* album that was released in limited edition to mark my 25 years in showbusiness and contained reworks of the rock classics *Lucille*, *Teddy Bear* and *Move It*.

Cliff Richard ★ 145

With a furry friend at Dreamworld in 1988.

When Phil Everly had kindly agreed to appear on the BBC documentary I, in return, agreed to work with him on his solo album, recorded in Britain and released in the spring of 1983. The producer was Stuart Colman, who'd made a string of hit records with artists such as Shakin' Stevens. Phil and I were to sing on *She Means Nothing To Me*, which was released as a single. This was a particularly rewarding project as, being my 25th year in showbusiness, it was a timely opportunity to work with one of the great star names from the other side of the Atlantic during my first years in the music business. We recorded at Eden Studios and the result was a real belter of a rock song which reached number nine in the charts.

As a sort of Christmas present to myself that year I planned to make my debut at my first Pro-celebrity tennis tournament in Brighton. It was not as well attended as subsequent tournaments, but it was a start and, I felt, a real sense of achievement.

During the first half of the eighties I toured Australia, the Far East, Scandinavia, South Africa and America and continued with a British gospel tour every year. Fortunately I was also be able to make two more field trips which helped me stay in touch with Tear Fund – a week in Kenya in 1982 and a fortnight in Haiti two years later. I narrated two films – *Cliff In Kenya* and *It's A Small World*. Both trips were humbling experiences, but there were some lighter moments and I remember making a group of Masai women dissolve into giggles when I played them some rock 'n' roll on an acoustic guitar.

My next project with a difference began with a conversation with Dave Clark about a science fiction musical, *Time*, which Dave had co–written and was keen to produce.

'I wanted to write a musical which shows that most of the bad things in life are caused through envy, bitterness and greed, and unless you get yourself in order you are in no position to put the world in order. It's a story about caring,' said Dave. 'There's a song that says, It's In every one of us to be wise. I believe that all gods are one and everyone should have the right to believe in a way that is right for them.'

Although I didn't fully agree with Dave's view, the musical contained a lot of truths and, after a lot of discussions with Dave, decided that I would be happy to appear in the show if we could make a few theological amendments.

We opened in April 1986 at the Dominion Theatre and the critics were scathing, but we sold 700,000 tickets. It was very unusual for me to be working in the same London theatre for a year. I made some good friends among the cast and even persuaded some of them to come with me to the David Lloyd Tennis Centre after the show for a midnight game of tennis.

Of all my albums around that time the one I always felt did far less well than it might have was *The Rock Connection*. I produced it with Keith Bessey, formerly my sound engineer, and it only reached number 43 in the charts. I didn't brood or analyse why it had

Appearing live on stage still gives me the biggest buzz. Everything about a live concert is still what I dreamed it would be like forty years ago.

There are times when I feel such great warmth from audiences. I stop and chat far too much, but it's as if I'm among friends!

Cliff

Cliff Richard

A Celebration

not been too well received, because I was too involved in working on the next album.

Alan Tarney told David Bryce that he would like to produce a definitive Cliff Richard album, choc full of hits and of a more consistent style than my recent albums, which sounded a great idea to me, so we began work on *Always Guaranteed* while I was working on *Time*.

Alan liked to work on his own early in the morning, strumming the guitar, recording a snatch of a new melody. I would go into the studio for four hours every afternoon to record vocals then take off for the Dominion Theatre. The result was one of my best albums ever, from which came all my hit singles for 1987 and the first of 1988. It was also a commercially successful album, with sales of more than 1.3 million copies. My next album, *Private Collection*, featured the best recordings from 1979-1988 and hit number one in the album charts, then came *Stronger*, with Alan Tarney creating most of the instrumentals and including four tracks which became hit singles.

Left: Time: The Musical was a very interesting project for me that was co-written by Dave Clark. Below: Reunited with the Shadows – thirty years on!

I can be a little trainspotterish about chart positions, but it seems to me quite natural in my line of business. For example my 100th single was *The Best Of Me*, released in 1989. It reached number two in UK singles chart. Oh, and I also became the first British artist to release 100 singles. Perhaps that's why I remember that one.

★

What a sensational close to the decade — at *The Event* on June 16, 1989 I faced my largest audience ever — 72,000 for each of two nights at Wembley Stadium. I had promised my fans an event, not just a show, and I don't think they were disappointed. When the tickets sold out for the first date over a single weekend, Mel Bush, the promoter, took the gamble of a second concert the following night, which also sold out. The Wembley concerts were a massive undertaking and a big risk. Ninety artists were involved and there were six weeks of rehearsals at Shepperton Studios.

The night before the show I was so charged with adrenalin I hardly got a wink of

In 1987 Madame Tussaud's asked me to do a 'sitting' for a new me.

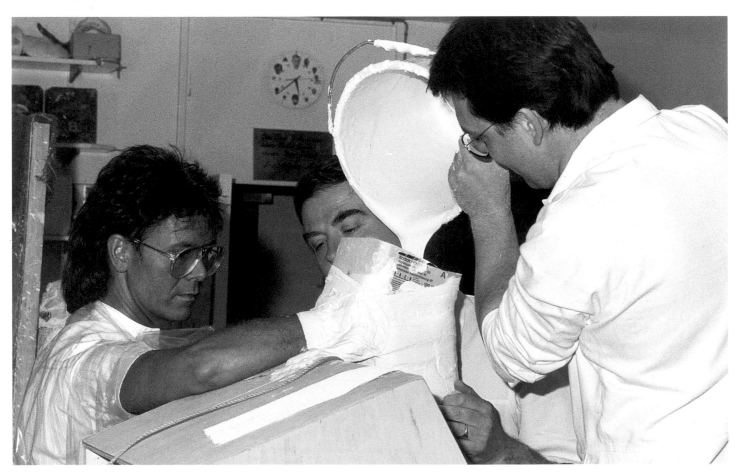

Left: Another proud moment for my mother and I was when I was presented with this gold disc at Claridges in London in 1988.
Below: With HRH Princess Anne at the Joy to the World event.

sleep – it's not like me to be apprehensive but this was a whopper!

The Dallas Boys and The Vernon Girls had reformed, looking great, for the show. The *Oh Boy!* band held the dance sets together, The Kalin Twins had agreed to appear despite the odd events of 1958 when I'd upstaged them on their own tour, and – of course – Hank Marvin, Bruce Welch, Tony Meehan and Jet Harris played on *Move It*.

The show opened with a trip down memory lane to recreate the mood of my first television appearance on *Oh Boy!* in 1958. MC Jimmy Henney walked out on stage and said: 'This is how it all began thirty years ago...' The band played the first chords of Buddy Holly's *Oh Boy*, the Dallas Boys stepped out in red bomber jackets, and then I danced out in my 1958 signature outfit of pink jacket, black shirt, black trousers and pink socks. The Vernon Girls, all still lithe and trim, swirled around in petticoats and shorts and for the last verse the Kalin Twins walked on in black dinner jackets.

Next we rocked straight into the Jerry Lee Lewis hit, *Whole Lotta Shakin*. By the time I was singing the Everly Brothers' *Bird Dog* with the Kalins and then off into Elvis's *Let's Have A Party*, I felt I was having a real party myself, enjoying every second and looking forward to the next eight great songs with the Shadows.

My final entrance was pretty spectacular – I strode on stage through clouds of dry ice wearing a made-to-measure white suit studded with two thousand diamantes. I wanted the sparkle to reach each one of the 72,000 in the audience!

The crowd was brilliant, all ready to join in and rock in their seats or where they stood and at the end of the show I could hardly hold back the tears. I've been criticised for speaking about God at my concerts many times, but this felt like the perfect moment. It seemed as if great waves of affection were rolling over me from the crowd and I wanted to give them something in return. I always feel that I have one thing to offer that is of any value, and that is the message that God exists, that Jesus is alive and He is yours if you want Him. That is what I told the Wembley crowd, then sang two gospel songs – *God Put A Fighter In Me* by Graham Kendrick and *Thief In The Night* by Paul Field.

The Event closed with *From A Distance*. Everything had gone perfectly. I could not have asked for more. And that night I slept very well indeed.

Left: Herby and Hal Kalin did forgive me after the events of 1958, and it was a great pleasure to appear with them at Wembley in June 1989.

A Celebration

Singles

1980

Dreamin'/Dynamite

A Little Love/Keep On Looking

1981

Wired For Sound/Hold On

Daddy's Home/Shakin' All Over

The Only Way Out/Under The Influence

1982

Where Do We Go From Here?/Discovering

Little Town/Love And A Helping Hand/You,

Me And Jesus, True Love Ways/ Galdrel

(both with London Symphony Orchestra)

1983

Never Say Die/Lucille

Please Don't Fall In Love/Too Close To Heaven

Baby You're Dynamite/Ocean Deep

1984

Shooting From The Heart/Small World

Heart User/I Will Follow You

She's So Beautiful/She's So Beautiful (instrumental)

1985

It's In Every One Of Us/Alone (instrumental)

Born To Rock 'n' Roll/Law Of The Universe
(instrumental)

1986

My Pretty One/Love Ya

1987

Some People/One Time Lover Man

Remember me/Another Christmas Day.

Two Hearts/Yesterday, Today, Forever

1988

Mistletoe & Wine/Marmaduke

The Best Of Me/Move It

1989

I Just Don't have The Heart/Wide Open Space

Lean On You/Hey Mister

Albums

1980

I'm No Hero

Love Songs

1981

Wired For Sound

Now You See Me... Now You Don't

1982

Dressed For The Occasion

1983

Silver

Cliff And The Shadows

1984

The Rock Connection

Always Guaranteed

1987

Private Collection

1988

Stronger

The Nineties

As I celebrate my fortieth
year in the music business, the
biggest thrill for me is Heathcliff.
I still live that experience;
it is part of my present, the
realisation of a lifelong dream.
I can't see how I'll ever
top it – unless of course I find
myself another musical.
Let the critics whinge.
There will always be
unimaginative people who say,
'Stick to what you know.'
Now why should I do that?

There was one particular moment in each performance of *Heathcliff* when I stood in the wings while the guitarist Gordon Giltrap played a darkly beautiful part of the Overture. Night after night as I waited for those few still seconds I used to thank God for letting me be there. That calmed me and, although I know it's hard to believe, I never felt nerves during any of the shows. Anxious in rehearsals, maybe, in the real-time *Heathcliff*, no – it was a joy!

Bringing together drama and music, this was my lifetime's dream come true. For me *Heathcliff* is the peak of my career so far. I enjoyed the whole experience so much that I don't think I could top it in terms of personal satisfaction. Had I been younger, might I have let the critics' dogged cynicism dull my enthusiasm? No, I think not.

To play the role of *Heathcliff* was a long-held ambition of mine. *Wuthering Heights* was the last book I remember reading in school and the emotion of the story really hooked me. Coincidentally, someone recently showed me some early press cuttings from the time I was making my first films – a journalist had asked me who I would like to play if ever I had the chance of a serious acting role. I'd answered without hesitation: Heathcliff.

When I finally decided the time was right for me to be involved in a full-scale musical, in 1992, I phoned the only director I knew – Frank Dunlop. He tried to talk me out of it at first; our conversation went something like this…

'*Wuthering Heights* is such a complicated story,' said Frank. 'Nobody has every made a really successful version of it, even the film with Sir Laurence Olivier couldn't lift it out of romantic pap. You've mentioned this idea so many times, but I can't see it working.'

'I know all that Frank, You're right,' I told him. 'But I happen to love the original novel. The character of Heathcliff fascinates me. I want to play that character.'

My director was not yet convinced about the project: 'But the whole story is full of hateful characters. There's not one who's truly lovable …'

'Please, anything you say. Let me do this. I really want to do this. Let's talk over dinner.' At times my persuading resembled pleading but I knew I would have to be ready to face opposition all along the line if I was to pursue this particular dream.

I'd been talking the idea over with Frank Dunlop for years and years, and I could understand his being a bit cagey about it because he was right in insisting that the story had never been very successfully adapted. In fact it wasn't until we got involved in looking at the book together that we both realised to what extent Heathcliff was the main character, a very solidly drawn personality with the stature of a mythological figure, a Machiavelli or even a Hamlet. And it was Frank's idea to work on the story not of *Wuthering Heights* but of Heathcliff and of the people that touched his life and the people he damaged.

Frank felt as I did that this should be a horrible, shocking story because the main character is evil. *Wuthering Heights* was a very down-to-earth and daring book for its time and frightened everyone who read it, and the Olivier film is to some extent a distortion of the story because of its romanticism.

The role of Heathcliff had been a long-held ambition for me. Wuthering Heights was the last book I remember reading at school, and it made a huge impression on me.

Cliff Richard

⭐ 161

The one thing that most women, if not all women, love about Heathcliff is that he was obsessive about one woman. He loved Cathy to the exclusion of all others.

Cliff

I also felt that everybody could identify with the emotions behind Heathcliff's fateful behaviour. Fortunately most of us get over the breakdown of a relationship, the fact that a loved one leaves us, that we are betrayed in some way by someone close to us, but Heathcliff made no attempt to get over his heartbreak or look for another relationship. The one thing that most women, if not all women, love about Heathcliff is that he was obsessive about one woman. He loved Cathy to the exclusion of all others.

Whenever Frank and I were in London we'd meet up and talk through our ideas, then it was a matter of finding, very importantly, the person who would write the music and lyrics.

Tim Rice was always top of my list, as one of the best lyricists alive today. There was a running joke between Tim and me that I never did any of his songs. All I could do was shrug my shoulders and say I'd get to do one soon, so it was fortunate for me that Tim now found this project interesting. He was intrigued about my keenness to portray someone fairly unpleasant and also had faith in the plot: 'If you've got a great story and you tell it tolerably well, that's what matters,' he said.

By the time Frank and I sat down to dinner with Tim Rice at the Langham Hilton in May 1993, we were talking business. We'd marked pages of the book where we needed songs and the result was that Tim's lyrics are very close to the text, in fact one of the songs actually starts with words straight from the book: 'It shall seem like a dream tomorrow,' (which Cathy says to Heathcliff when he comes back to her from his fortune-hunting travels). We agreed that we needed no pretty, light songs about the beauty of the Yorkshire moors, but songs of fierce passions, about extreme love, extreme jealousy and extreme emotional cruelty – every song concerns emotions!

When John Farrar agreed to write the music I had my dream team. Frank didn't know John, but I went on and on about how great he is. When Frank met him and heard his work he agreed that John has an extraordinarily open mind as a musician. John wrote the hit songs from Grease – *You're The One That I Want* and *Totally Devoted To You* – and I'd always felt he has a very individual talent that made his rock 'n' roll music different.

With Tim Rice in London and John Farrar in Los Angeles there was a lot of hot fax collaboration. John would write tunes he felt appropriate to the lyrics and found he enjoyed the idea of having more freedom in writing for a musical than for a strictly pop album.

Olivia Newton-John played the part of Cathy Earnshaw for the *Heathcliff* album; it was remarkable reunion for her because she's known John since she was 16 and used to sing with his wife Pat, including vocal backing for me in the early days. Making the video for the album was a real pleasure. I had no problems looking into Olivia's eyes, nor she into mine, as we already had an affinity and that really counts when you're trying to bring out some kind of emotion.

The album *Songs From Heathcliff* was released in October 1995 and given so little airplay that after seeing the show fans were asking if the music was coming out on an

With Tim Rice, who wrote the wonderful lyrics for the show and Helen Hobson, who I felt immediately would make the perfect Cathy.

A Celebration

After only one week of rehearsals for the stage musical I knew the project was going to be very demanding of me. I remember thinking, 'The only way to succeed is to know everything backwards.'

Cliff

Cliff Richard

Helen Hobson was one of the 'dream team' that made Heathcliff such a great milestone for me.

album – and that was over a year after it had been released! I heard a fantastic statistic once – a record of mine is played somewhere in Britain every 20 minutes, and that makes me believe that the *Heathcliff* music deserved to be given a chance on radio, if only on the strength of what I've done in the past. And if people didn't like it they wouldn't buy it. Surely one DJ might have given me two weeks' airplay and then, if the record failed, said, 'Sorry, Cliff, but it's bye bye to that one.' However, by the time the show opened I was beyond worrying about radio DJs and narrow-casting policies. I'm heartened by the existence of International Cliff Week when fans evidently bombard radio stations with requests for my songs to be played, which is a lovely chuckle, even if the stations still ignore me.

It was a humbling experience watching so many talented performers audition for roles in *Heathcliff* at the Old Vic theatre. Auditions are awfully unpredictable things. I don't know how actors cope with them – you can do so much work at home but it's difficult to predict how it will go on the day.

Watching Helen Hobson auditioning, I had a strong feeling that she would be right for Cathy. She could do everything, looked fantastic, has a wonderful singing voice in a wide range of styles, and has that natural English-rose look I'd always imagined Cathy to have. Helen was wearing her hair in long Titian curls for the audition, and I found out later she had stood by a window to let her hair blow in the wind to get that just-off-the-moors look!

I went over to say hello to her afterwards and Roger from my office said he'd noticed us speaking together and thought we looked right – always a good sign.

After only one week of rehearsals for the stage musical I knew the project was going to be very demanding of me. I remember thinking, 'The only way to succeed is to know everything backwards.' We began rehearsals in rooms at the English Folk Dance and Song Society, and any nerves the cast and I had about each other disappeared as it quickly became clear that we had a good blend of talents. Singing harmonies with people means you have got to get very close very quickly and there's a bonding that comes about through the music. What I had to concentrate on was letting the lyrics become second nature so that I could sing every section without having to think, 'What's the next track?'

I had already read *Wuthering Heights* a dozen times and had a hand in choosing all the dialogue straight from the novel. Every night I would read the sections of the novel we were working on for the show and after about a month I felt so comfortable in the part I didn't worry about it any more. Frank gave me an important key to the stage performance when he said: 'If you are prepared to make a fool of yourself in rehearsals, you'll be all right.'

I knew what he meant. In a dramatic musical when you think that you know exactly what you have to do you need go that much further. If you think you're weeping loudly you've got to scream. And I did.

I remember seeing a photograph of Patrick Brontë, Emily Brontë's father, sitting in an armchair. He looked like George Bernard Shaw did just before he died – white-haired, long

In a dramatic musical when you think that you know exactly what you have to do you need to go that much further. If you think you're weeping loudly you've got to scream. And I did.

Cliff

Cliff Richard

Many people thought I wouldn't be able to play the part convincingly because of my 'Mr Nice Guy' image. Luckily the audiences didn't seem to agree with them!

white beard and deep, wise eyes. The caption said 'Patrick Brontë at the age of 56'. So I thought, I'm 56 now. I've lived the life I've wanted to live and I'm ready for the emotional depth of this character, who would be considered a very mature man at the age of 38, the age Emily Brontë made him.

Many people died in their teens in the early 19th century. Emily lived long enough to see her poetry accepted in literary circles, but she never saw the great success of her novel *Wuthering Heights*. She died at 30 of tuberculosis (as did her sister Anne at 29, and Charlotte died in childbirth a 39). I was fascinated by the emotional intensity of their lives, which now seem so brief, and I wanted the musical to reflect that with a string of strong, emotional songs.

At the press launch one journalist suggested that I was too old to play the part of Heathcliff. For years newspapers have told me that I don't look my age and now they were saying I was too old to play Heathcliff! Looking in the mirror I felt that at 56 I was the perfect person in this country to play a 38-year-old.

One journalist said, 'I can't imagine you stomping around home in a bad temper. It must be your image.'

'That's good,' I replied. 'I wouldn't like to see you go around thinking of me in that way.'

If someone gives an actor a knife and says every night for the next six months they have to stab Julius Caesar with hate and venom, the actor does it happily; it doesn't mean they do it at home! It was hard to understand why the journalist didn't ask himself, how come such a successful director as Frank Dunlop is involved? How come Jo Vanek with an amazing background in production design, Andrew Bridge who lights all the best shows in town, and, of course, Sir Tim Rice are involved. Would they do this if they thought I couldn't cut the mustard? Of course not!

Having gone double gold with the album without the aid of any radio airplay, I could only assume that once we got on the road and people started coming to see the show, they would realise we were trying to do something a little bit different. But I knew these preconceived ideas of many music and theatre critics were fixed. My real-life character is unlike that of Heathcliff so the general feeling seemed to be that I would be unconvincing – and this before anyone had seen the show.

Although I can't say that when I was a child I was mistreated by an older brother and I have never been cruelly cast aside by a lover for someone else, I have nevertheless felt and lost love, wished someone else had loved me. We've all experienced those kind of feelings and that's where the drama lies. Yet the national press had written me off as Heathcliff right through the planning stages, which was virtually a promise of despicable reviews however good the show finally turned out to be.

Tim Rice encouraged us all by saying that the ideas for all his best shows had been rubbished, including the planning of *Evita*. Meanwhile Frank sometimes got annoyed at the

The cast were distraught with nerves and I kept saying to them, 'This is just a rehearsal. The people out there are all friends and relations. Nobody there is out to get us – no press. We can just have a great time.'
And we did.

bad press: 'It's really unfair to criticise a performance before it happens. They've already written that you can't do it, won't do it, shouldn't do it, before we've even got the music and the script together and started stage rehearsals!'

Nevertheless we remained optimistic and happy with the project. I had steeled myself for bad reviews and become hardened to the jibes of people who had been vindictive and vicious towards me in the five years leading up to our opening. I spent two moments thinking about the press then I thought, to hell with them.

I still can't believe I did the whole thing without any nerves. The first night we performed to an audience was the dress rehearsal. The cast were distraught with nerves and I kept saying to them, 'This is just a rehearsal. The people out there are all friends and relations. Nobody there is out to get us – no press. We can just have a great time.' And we did.

So when we opened for real in Birmingham Academy in October 1996 I went on stage thinking, 'Never mind the critics. We'll let our audiences be the judge' and I was absolutely confident we'd created something audiences would enjoy. My responsibility was to that audience and they responded with great warmth (even though 60 or so of my biggest fans had braved night-time sub-zero temperatures in an improvised village of 13 tents to queue for tickets for the première). So many people had said I couldn't play the part because I'm a Mr Nice Guy that it was particularly enjoyable to feel so different when I looked in the mirror after I had donned the wig and the make up.

At the start of the first show my eyes filled with tears of happiness. The audience was wonderfully responsive and when we got to the end of the first half, I was looking forward to seeing their reaction to the dramatic spiral that was still to come. At the curtain call everyone in the audience seemed to be throwing white carnations. I have to say that night was the biggest buzz I've ever felt, the combination of singing the music and being surrounded by actors is exhilarating.

I was a little apprehensive about the start of our second run, at the Edinburgh Playhouse. People would have read the scathing reviews and we'd only sold 40 per cent of the tickets there. However, I needn't have worried. Within a week of opening in Edinburgh we were sold out and that told me one thing: nobody really listens to a critic if they hear a different opinion from a friend or by word of mouth. We extended our run in Edinburgh by about two weeks and went on to play to packed audiences at the Manchester Palace Theatre and London's Labbatt's Apollo in Hammersmith.

Heathcliff played to nearly half a million people, broke even in six months and played for seven and a half months, so we made some money as well. There were £5 million's worth of advance bookings – that's more than *Phantom* or *Cats* and probably the highest advanced booking for any show in the last 25 years. The video was the most successful one of my career, in the top ten for more than six months, again with hardly any positive publicity except for word-of-mouth recommendations from people who had seen the show.

That first night in Birmingham in October 1996 was the biggest buzz I've ever felt, the combination of singing the music and being surrounded by actors is exhilarating.

Cliff

Wherever I go I meet some wonderful people who never fail to raise a smile. I'm not sure, but I think these two ladies were offering me a lift!

I definitely didn't go into the production thinking I might break any records, so when woke up one morning and read that we'd broken all the box office records for the first day of booking in the West End I said to myself, 'Eek! Now we've got to do it!'

Heathcliff is certainly going to be my main gauge of success from now on.

My involvement with *Heathcliff* has coloured this decade very strongly so far, but neither that nor any other new performing territory I can explore is likely to stop me from recording and touring, as these have become my way of life.

In 1990 I had the honour of appearing at the London Palladium for the Queen Mother's 90th Birthday Concert, and also the pleasure of celebrating my own fiftieth birthday at a great after-show party in Birmingham. Back home I held a theme party in a marquee on my lawn, where everyone dressed up as they were in 1958.

In the same year we broke all previous records for Wembley Arena when 216,000 people came to concerts over 18 nights, (during which I was able to take part in a live link-up in tribute to *Coronation Street*). My double album *From A Distance: The Event Live* was released in November 1990, followed by a Christmas number one with *Saviour's Day*.

I thought *Saviour's Day* a better song than *Mistletoe & Wine* but it didn't capture the public imagination in the same way – whereas *Mistletoe & Wine* sold a million copies in four weeks, *Saviour's Day* got to number one but I don't think it sold much more than half a million. The competition was a rap song, so I suppose that just happened to be the year for a Christmas rap.

It's true that I'd been enjoying some large audiences, but it struck me as amusing to read in1991 that *The Sunday Times* magazine ranked me among Britain's 200 richest people (I just scraped in). My business manager, Malcolm Smith, dropped me a note which read, 'Don't spend it because I haven't found it yet.'

On the *Access All Areas* tour in 1992 I played to audiences totalling some 480,000, with *Cliff Richard: The Album* and *Access All Areas* both making number ones in the album and video ratings. All of which sounds pretty showbizzy, but, although such successes are a great thrill, I value my private life more and more. I still absolutely love the amazing high I get from performing to a huge audience and I still value my friends outside the music business and our precious lazy holidays spent sunbathing, playing tennis and listening to music.

When I decided to try skiing – I hadn't found the time until I was 50 – I went to Lech in Austria and enjoyed the challenge. After six ski trips I've just managed to get the hang of parallel turns, and Lech has indoor tennis courts. What more could I ask for?

The first time I went to Lech, Prince Charles was there with Princess Diana and their children, then the following year Diana was there with friends and the children. She would

There's no place like home.

Cliff Richard

walk into the hotel from the slopes and flop down, laughing, on a large settee. I remember one day she flopped down between two little girls and gave them a cuddle. They all had a giggle, and I don't think the children had any idea who she was, other than the friendly mother of two children of her own. She was also a woman who would take her sons to visit hospitals in the dark of night to avoid publicity, and yet she was often accused of manipulating the press. As if anyone could.

The next time we stayed in the same hotel I knew Diana at a sort of social level and she knew that I always brought along a guitar and would sometimes strum a few tunes in the bar with everyone signing along.

When Princess Diana asked me if I would sing in the bar for her boys, I happily agreed and when the appointed evening arrived I started singing some of my better known stuff such as *Summer Holiday* and *Living Doll*. Prince William and Prince Harry were sitting with a couple of young friends and appeared to me to be listening in a rather gentlemanly way, probably trying hard to stifle yawns.

Then Harry made a request: 'I say, do you know *Great Balls Of Fire*?'

'Well, I know it.' I had to smile. 'But how come you know it?'

It turned out that Princess Diana had given them an album of rock legends. The princes knew quite a lot of old rock 'n' roll and really liked it. So *Great Balls Of Fire* it was, and with vigour… Both William and Harry started dancing immediately, WIlliam in a stylish and controlled manner with the sort of regal arm movements one might expect from a future monarch, and Harry? Picking up a Toblerone packet which became his microphone, he went wild! With a mixture of his own uninhibited dancing style and a few movements that looked as if they'd been copied from Michael Jackson, Prince Harry bopped the night away. The young princes clearly loved rock 'n' roll. I can't wait to be able to ask the princes when they're grown up if they remember my first Royal Command performance for them!

Left: Live at Wembley in 1994.
Below: Sampling some of the finer things at the Hampton Court Flower Show in 1994. It's always a very enjoyable event.

My home in Portugal is a very special place for me. I go out there whenever I can find the time for some rest and relaxation.

As I flew back to England from Portugal on the weekend that my knighthood was to be announced in 1995, I said to my friends, 'Supposing the Queen decides it's been some kind of a mistake? Perhaps they would revise the list.'

I'd been officially informed, but hadn't let myself think about it too much until that homeward bound flight. After we landed and were walking through the airports I noticed an unusual number of press photographers waiting and I thought, 'Yes, I really have got a knighthood!'

Many people expect performers to be unfazed by any kind of public appearance, but receiving a knighthood is, I suppose, a very traditional and formal performance. And it's something you can't plan; you can plan a campaign for an album and hope it gets gold and platinum awards, but my knighthood just came as a wonderful surprise.

I was invested as Knight Bachelor at 10.30am in Buckingham Palace on October 25, 1995. The Queen did not say, 'Arise Sir Cliff', but had to wield an enormous sword for dubbing on both shoulders. When she stepped back and passed the sword to an attendant I had to stand up from the kneeling position, with the help of a sort of handle attached to the comfy kneeler, then lean forward as The Queen put over my head the ribbon of the Knight Bachelor. I can't remember what I said ... I was quite emotional and babbling. The same sword must have knighted Olivier and so many other greats!

Cliff Richard   ✳ 179

I was invested as Knight Bachelor at 10.30 am in Buckingham Palace on October 25, 1995. The Queen did not say, 'Arise Sir Cliff', but had to wield an enormous sword for dubbing on both shoulders.

Cliff

Cliff Richard ⋆ 181

The celebrations for the 50th anniversary of VE Day were extraordinary. There was a wonderful atmosphere at Hyde Park for the concert, and a great warmth emanated from the huge crowd.

After the ceremony I said to my sisters, 'I feel such a fool. The Queen is probably thinking to herself that she should have given this to a doctor, or at least someone who could talk, because I really don't remember saying anything coherent!'

'Oh, you were talking for ages!' they said – which didn't help.

A knighthood is a very great honour. However I think the 'Sir' affects other people more than it does me. It can be strangely distancing in that I can see some people are uncomfortable about what to call me, and a few even look as if they want to bow or something. It seems ridiculous that anyone can feel that way about me, an ordinary flesh and blood person.

Another occasion that made me stop and think hard about the relationship of past and present was the 50th anniversary celebrations of VE Day. It was a beautiful summer Saturday in London and a wonderful atmosphere at the Hyde Park Concert. I'd never in my life wished I'd been part of the Second World War or any war for that matter, so like many others of the post-war generation, I felt a little separate from the celebrations at first. I was aware that there were a lot of people partying who had survived the war, but what could one say if one hadn't lived through the horror, how could I presume to imagine the myriad difficulties of their youth?

When I sat down and thought about what I was going to say on stage, I thought of what a different world, a completely different England there would be if our forefathers

Above: In December 1997 I sang at the Children in Crisis concert, yet another event that made me stop and think.
Left: Singing outside Buckingham Palace after the 50th anniversary of VE Day. Dame Vera Lynn and Sir Harry Secombe sang too, with Bob Holness as compere.

hadn't fought for our freedom. I've read it a million times, but on this day I really felt it in my heart.

I'd been invited to sing outside the Palace on the following Monday, with Sir Harry Secombe and Dame Vera Lynn, and Bob Holness as compere. To get on to the little podium outside the palace gates we walked through a crowd of senior citizens and they were reaching across and touching Dame Vera, saying, 'Oh God bless you, thank you.'

The Queen, the Queen Mother and Princess Margaret came out on to the palace balcony and when a display of noisy planes swooped over one could almost feel the memories of the crowd, of the days of loss, fear and then victory. I'm sure that thousands of people born after the war felt, as I did, a focus of realisation and a deep gratitude to so many of their elders.

In January 1997 I met up with the man who was to help shape the sound of my fortieth anniversary album. I liked Peter Wolf and his wife Michelle fron the first time we had dinner together, The three of us got on really well – I liked them instantly and that is so important when you are considering working with people day in and day out in the studio.

Peter's first question was, 'What direction do you feel you ought to go in with your next album?'

I've heard that question many times before and I have a stock answer: 'If we find ten great songs they will tell us what direction we're going in and how they should be done.'

I'm not interested in limiting an album by specifying a certain type of sound before we start work on it. For my latest album *Real*, we had 18 really fantastic songs and we could only put 12 or 13 on the album. They are really diverse, perhaps leaning towards rhythm and blues, but also some beautiful ballads, one being *Butterfly Kisses*. And I get to do a fantastic duet with an opera singer Vincenzo La Scola – now had we been talking about a fixed direction I probably wouldn't have ended up singing with him.

Peter Wolf's style of production is the lynchpin, the factor that gives the album cohesion. As I write this I'm sure that we've just finished making the best album I've ever recorded... but I guess I always feel like that when I've made a new album.

I started planning my fortieth year celebrations well in advance – my career started five years before most of the big rock 'n' roll names in this country, and in that respect the Beatles and the Rolling Stones are never going to catch up with me!

My fortieth anniversary tour began on the other side of the world in New Zealand. We planned something very special for fans in Australia and New Zealand – a concert with a 60-piece orchestra and my own band, performed in the round with the stage in the middle of the hall, which I've never done before. At first I couldn't see how it would work because one hundred per cent of the time half the audience can't see my face. So how could I feel I

Left: With Darren Day at the Summer Holiday party in July 1997 – only 35 years after the real thing!

Cliff Richard

A Celebration

was singing directly to them all? I found rehearsals difficult at first because there seemed to be no focal point and, of course, there would be no light show as we had no backdrop. But it was different – more intimate, with a feeling that everyone is close to the stage – and I realised that the public responded differently, too.

Performing in Australia is always great for me because over the years I've been lucky enough to win many loyal fans whose tastes I feel I know very well. Many artists resist singing their old stuff believing that only a new sound is valid, even though it's the music that's gone before that attracts the audience. So I blended together a group of songs that I know have been hits in Australia and if they weren't hits for me they are songs I admire which were hits for someone else.

In the middle of the stage was a two-way revolving platform which worked very well for a number I sang with Olivia Newton-John. We'd stand shoulder-to-shoulder, looking out at the audience in opposite directions so that as we revolved people always had one of us facing them – that was a great new experience.

In Australia I played to more people than I did on my previous tour and that's the only way I can gauge my success. Whereas, in the UK, winter is the season for concert-goers, in Australia it's the hot summer months when everyone loves to be out on river trips, picnics or listening to music – which makes touring Australia doubly pleasurable. I came home having played to 200,000 people and thought to myself, gosh that's a fantastic percentage of the Australian population of about 16 million.

The shows are timed and these Australian ones turned out to be the longest I've ever done, even though I'd kept the same number of songs. The reason was that I just couldn't resist chatting with the audience and the chatty bits added up to about half an hour each evening! I didn't mean to do that, and resolved that in London I'd sing extra songs and talk less.

★

Many artists resist singing their old stuff believing that only a new sound is valid, even though it's the music that's gone before that attracts the audience.

Cliff

Postscript 1999

★

Attending the charity gala to celebrate the twentieth anniversary of Grease the musical.

Because it would be a shame to miss out the last year of the century from my story, I'm adding a final chapter to bring you up to the new millennium. I shall remember 1999 for some fantastic experiences, especially during my Fortieth Anniversary concerts and the Route of Kings Concert in Hyde Park in July – and to top all that, the momentous Countdown to the Millennium concerts in Birmingham. There have also been some devastating moments of sadness and a time of deep reflection when I decided to take a twelve-month break in the year 2000.

For me a very important part of marking my forty years in the music business was the series of Royal Albert Hall concerts – in November and December 1998 and March 1999. This was the first time I'd performed in the round at the RAH and, as I appeared on a rising platform in the centre of the circular stage to sing *From a Distance*, I was given a fabulous welcome. With the Royal Philharmonic Concert Orchestra to accompany me I had the chance to sing a wide variety of songs, including some surprises, but mostly songs I've loved all my life.

I've had a lot of good fortune with the records I've released, as I don't write them myself, and over the years I've been given some beautiful songs to sing. But I suppose there's only one word to describe my attitude to songs – greedy! I sometimes hear other people's songs and I think, why didn't they ask *me* to do that? For my Fortieth Anniversary Concerts I had the luxury of choosing some of my favourite pop ballads, including *Will You Still Love Me Tomorrow* and *Softly As I Leave You*. I am very proud to say that Matt Monro said the version I recorded was the *second* best he'd ever heard!

For the finale of the Royal Albert Hall concerts we sang *Peace in Our Time* with about seventy fine musicians in total making music on and around the stage. The atmosphere was electric and I felt surrounded by friends. The three guest singers I introduced at the Royal Albert Hall are all relatively new friends – Vincenzo la Scola (with whom I sang *Vita Mia*), young Barratt Waugh and Michelle Wolf.

Michelle did the backing vocals on *Real As I Wanna Be*, which was recorded at the studio in the beautiful Austrian home she shares with her husband Peter Wolf. I don't think I've ever recorded an album in more conducive surroundings – they made me feel so welcome.

One morning I woke up early to the smell of coffee, the sound of Peter tinkling

I shall remember 1999 for some fantastic experiences, especially during my Fortieth Anniversary concerts and the Route of Kings Concert in Hyde Park in July.

Cliff

Cliff Richard

A very important part of marking my forty years in the music business was the series of Royal Albert Hall concerts — in November and December 1998 and March 1999. This was the first time I'd performed in the round at the RAH and, as I appeared on a rising platform in the centre of the circular stage to sing From A Distance, I was given a fabulous welcome. With the Royal Philharmonic Concert Orchestra to accompany me I had the chance to sing a wide variety of songs, including some surprises, but mostly songs I've loved all my life.

Cliff

Dolled up for Royal Ascot during the 1999
Ascot racing festival.

A Celebration

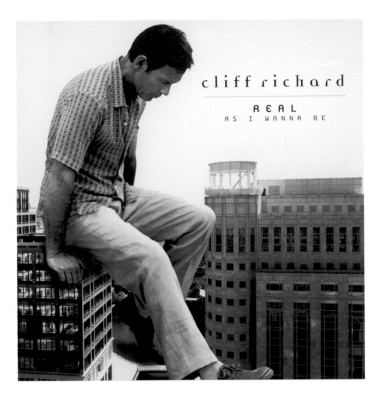

Real As I Wanna Be, the album I recorded with Michelle and Peter Wolf in the beautiful surroundings of their Austrian home.

about on the piano and Michelle's footsteps across the floor – carrying a tray of coffees to the piano top, I guessed. I showered and went down to join them. It was as if the crisp clear sunshine streaming through the windows had woken us all up early with the purpose of inspiring a song. A long day stretched before us, with no appointments to keep except to make music and we wrote a song together, which is now one of my favourites. It is the song I sang with Michelle at the Royal Albert Hall concert – *She Makes Me Feel Like a Man*.

The Royal Albert Hall concerts were sold out and I was presented with an award for the greatest number of sell-out solo performances at that illustrious venue by the Chief Executive, David Elliot. Sales of the video of the concert also broke records, but I had been disappointed at the lack of radio air-play given to the *Real As I Wanna Be* album. Those stupid radio rules about my being too old to listen to were annoying me again.

I became so incensed by this ageism that I invented an *alter ego* with a ridiculous name and released a re-mixed version of *Can't Keep This Feeling In*. My air-time-worthy pseudonym was Blacknight. This version, I thought, would be more likely to appeal to DJs because it was more dance orientated than the original version and sounded like a young re-mix voice. The Blacknight record was distributed to all the DJs and gained some popularity with those who thought it was by a young unknown artist. I was genuinely surprised at how many people were fooled. And the Blacknight version did passably well; it even entered the singles charts for a few days in the low twenties somewhere.

In the creative spheres of the arts, theatre, design and humour, experience and

The Daily Mail unexpectedly leapt to my defence with a 'Save Sir Cliff' campaign. The newspaper even suggested that readers cut out a coupon to be posted to Chris in support of the Cliff Richard Preservation Society, demanding 'Lift Your Fatwa on Cliff'.

Save Sir Cliff

I was moved to tears, he says

AN emotional Sir Cliff Richard yesterday thanked his fans as support grew for the Mail's campaign to get his music back on the airwaves. The singer, who is considered too old by his radio critics, said the campaign had moved him to tears.

—— SEE PAGE 15 ——

NOW POST YOUR PROTEST...

From: The Cliff Richard Preservation Society. To: Chris Evans
The Mad Mullah of Pop, Virgin Radio, 1 Golden Square, London W1

LIFT YOUR FATWA ON CLIFF!

lasting popularity are considered of value. It is a fact that young people listen to less music than they used to – perhaps radio stations have something to do with that. Certainly the variety in popular music has always been one of the strengths of the British music industry and I don't think anyone is going to change that – not even the most ginger of DJs.

When the time came for my television interview with Chris Evans, I was ready to do battle on the subject. I relished the opportunity to air my views in public about the unfairness of radio stations refusing to play older artists and Chris made an amusing attempt to justify the system. The aftermath of that interview was even more fun.

Chris decided to publicly blacklist my records, along with a reported 240 other radio stations, and smashed copies of my old hits on his radio show. At the time my single with my own name on the label was in the top ten.

Game on: Ageing Ginger DJ v. Banned Ageing Cliff.

To bury the hatchet, Chris was reported to have offered to record a song with me if his listeners raised £1 million for Comic Relief. I won't be able to do it, but as far as I was concerned there was no hatchet to bury.

I took out an advert in *Music Week* headed 'Now Who's Breaking Records?' which listed great world events that have occurred during the last forty years, including, of course, my own record-breaking achievements. The man who helped me with the advert was Trevor Beattie, who created the racy 'Hello Boys!' Wonderbra advert; never let it be said that I don't look to the skills of more senior experts in publicity!

The *Daily Mail* unexpectedly leapt to my defence with a 'Save Sir Cliff' campaign. The newspaper even suggested that readers cut out a coupon to be posted to Chris in support of the Cliff Richard Preservation Society, demanding 'Lift Your Fatwa on Cliff'.

I felt like an ancient monument! But I knew my fans would respond, even without encouragement from the press. Letters came in by the sackful and the morning after the television show there had been a group of my fans protesting outside Chris Evans's broadcasting studio.

I was just happy to have the opportunity to publicise my gripe against ageism in music radio. The spirited interview with Chris and the hype that followed was all a piece of good rock 'n' roll merriment.

NOW WHO'S BREAKING RECORDS?

1958 SOBERS 365 CLIFF ELVIS DRAFTED·HI-FI INVENTED·FIRST JET PASSENGERS CROSS ATLANTIC 1959 HULA HOOP CLIFF MONKEYS IN SPACE·MINI LAUNCHED CLIFF BEN HUR OPENS 1960 PRINCESS MARGARET MARRIES CLIFF DEAD SEA SCROLLS CLIFF JFK PRESIDENT CLIFF 1961 E-TYPE JAGUAR CLIFF GAGARIN FIRST MAN IN SPACE CLIFF BAY OF PIGS CLIFF BERLIN WALL BUILT CLIFF 1962 DECCA REJECTS BEATLES CLIFF MARILYN DIES CLIFF MANDELA JAILED CLIFF 1963 WILSON PM CLIFF PROFUMO SCANDAL·LYNDON B.JOHNSON PRESIDENT CLIFF MARTIN LUTHER KING'S "DREAM" SPEECH CLIFF GREAT TRAIN ROBBERY CLIFF BEATLEMANIA·JFK SHOT 1964 CASSIUS CLAY WORLD CHAMP CLIFF MODS AND ROCKERS BATTLE ON THE BEACHES·VIETNAM WAR 1965 CHURCHILL DIES CLIFF BEATLES GET MBE'S CLIFF 1966 ENGLAND WIN WORLD CUP CLIFF 1967 SIX DAY WAR·SGT PEPPER RELEASED CLIFF FIRST HEART TRANSPLANT 1968 FOSBURY FLOP CLIFF MARTIN LUTHER KING SHOT·NIXON PRESIDENT 1969 CONCORDE FLIES·MAN ON MOON 1970 BOEING 747 ENTERS SERVICE·HEATH PM·BEATLES SPLIT 1971 DECIMALISATION·IDI AMIN·HOT PANTS AT ASCOT 1972 BRITAIN JOINS EEC·OLGA KORBUT WINS GOLD·TUTANKHAMUN 1973 WATERGATE CLIFF PRINCESS ANNE MARRIES·THREE DAY WEEK 1974 HAROLD WILSON PM·STREAKING·NIXON RESIGNS·LUCAN VANISHES 1975 NORTH SEA OIL FLOWS 1976 CALLAGHAN PM·CARTER PRESIDENT·SUMMER OF '76·SEX PISTOLS SWEAR ON TV 1977 SPACE SHUTTLE FLIES·RED RUM WINS 3RD NATIONAL·SILVER JUBILEE·LAKER SKY TRAIN·SATURDAY NIGHT FEVER 1978 AMOCO CADIZ OIL DISASTER·FIRST TEST TUBE BABY 1979 AYATOLLA RETURNS TO IRAN CLIFF THATCHER PM·MOTHER THERESA WINS NOBEL PEACE PRIZE 1980 SAS STORM IRANIAN EMBASSY CLIFF BORG WINS 5TH WIMBLEDON·LENNON SHOT 1981 CLIFF BRIXTON RIOTS·CHARLES AND DI MARRY CLIFF 1982 ERIKA ROE STREAKS AT RUGBY MATCH·DE LOREAN BANKRUPT·FALKLANDS WAR·ET 1983 FIRST ARTIFICIAL HEART·MICRO CHIP·THATCHER RE-ELECTED 1984 BOY GEORGE·TORVILL & DEAN PERFECT 6'S·MINERS STRIKE·MICHAEL JACKSON THRILLER·4 GOLDS FOR CARL LEWIS·BRIGHTON BOMB 1985 SINCLAIR C5·MIKHAIL GORBACHEV PRESIDENT·HEYSEL STADIUM·LIVE AID·MADONNA·TITANIC FOUND 1986 SPACE SHUTTLE EXPLODES CLIFF MARADONA "HAND OF GOD"·TYSON YOUNGEST HEAVY WEIGHT CHAMP CLIFF HALLEY'S COMET 1987 HERALD OF FREE ENTERPRISE SINKS CLIFF MATHIAS RUST LANDS IN RED SQUARE·UK HURRICANE·WALL ST·CRASH·SUNFLOWERS SELLS FOR £24,000,000 1988 PIPER ALPHA OIL RIG DISASTER CLIFF BEN JOHNSON SCANDAL·GEORGE BUSH PRESIDENT·LOCKERBIE DISASTER 1989 CLIFF BERLIN WALL FALLS 1990 MANDELA FREED·POLL TAX RIOTS·'GAZZA' CRIES·SADDAM INVADES KUWAIT CLIFF THATCHER OUSTED·MAJOR PM 1991 GULF WAR·JOHN MC CARTHY FREED·TERRY WAITE FREED·FREDDIE MERCURY DIES·GORBACHEV RESIGNS 1992 PADDY 'PANTSDOWN'·TYSON JAILED·CONSERVATIVES FOURTH WIN CLIFF·NIGEL MANSELL F1 CHAMP·CLINTON PRESIDENT·WINDSOR BURNS 1993 GRAND NATIONAL DECLARED VOID CLIFF ARAFAT & RABIN SHAKE HANDS 1994 MANDELA PRESIDENT·OJ SIMPSON TRIAL·CHANNEL TUNNEL CLIFF 1995 NICK LEESON BANKRUPTS BARINGS 1996 BLAIR PM 1997 LIFE ON MARS 1998 SMALL GINGER DJ REFUSES TO PLAY NEW CLIFF SINGLE. 18.10.98 'CAN'T KEEP THIS FEELING IN' ENTERS NETWORK SINGLES CHART AT NUMBER 10 ·'REAL AS I WANNA BE' ENTERS NETWORK ALBUM CHART AT NUMBER 8 FIVE DECADES ONE CLIFF

BLA(KNIGHT

Jill and I had become friends
after I put in a surprise
appearance as her partner at the
Viennese Opera Ball.

Cliff

The Real Tour, in April, took me to Germany, Austria and Denmark, where I received the shocking news of Jill Dando's murder. Like so many people who had loved Jill, I was devastated but unable to retreat or make sense of the tragedy.

Jill and I had become friends after I put in a surprise appearance as her partner at the Viennese Opera Ball. Jill had been involved in charity activities with Gloria Hunniford and myself, and for three years we had all met to celebrate birthdays and Christmas together. I was also hoping to participate in Jill and Alan's wedding ceremony this year. It was unthinkable that we should be attending the funeral of a young friend so full of life.

Jill had been involved in charity activities with Gloria Hunniford and myself, and for three years we had all met to celebrate birthdays and Christmas together. I was also hoping to participate in Jill and Alan's wedding ceremony this year. It was unthinkable that we should be attending the funeral of a young friend so full of life.

Cliff

Cliff Richard

A few months after Jill's funeral, Gloria Hunniford and I took part in the launch of the Jill Dando rose, in association with the British Heart Foundation, at the Hampton Court Flower Show. The rose is a fitting memorial to a radiantly beautiful person whom I respected enormously, and is especially poignant as Jill was a dedicated supporter of this charity. The rose that I have planted in my garden will keep her memory living and growing for me.

Cliff

A few months after Jill's funeral, Gloria Hunniford and I took part in the launch of the Jill Dando rose, in association with the British Heart Foundation, at the Hampton Court Flower Show. The rose is a fitting memorial to a radiantly beautiful person whom I respected enormously, and is especially poignant as Jill was a dedicated supporter of this charity. The rose that I have planted in my garden will keep her memory living and growing for me.

The final leg of my Real Tour was in Dublin and Belfast at the end of April. I love the buzz I get from audiences in Ireland — that Irish hospitality is always warm and welcoming, and I have some good friends I like to catch up with when I'm in Dublin.

My next major concerts were on the Route of Kings in Hyde Park in July. I was delighted to share the stage with Elaine

The eight solid days of rehearsing were all worthwhile when we got on stage in Hyde Park for the Route of Kings concerts in July.

A Celebration

the set had bright lights and palm trees and the singers were dressed almost as we did in Summer Holiday, in white T-shirts and tight pants. We wanted to create the atmosphere of a summer party, with lots of pop, and I was very happy with the upbeat result.

Cliff

I think the majority of people associate the start of the twenty-first century with renewal and would wish to see the new era celebrated by 'putting something back into the community'

Paige, whom I've admired for several years. We rehearsed for eight full, long days and performed before some 35,000 people over three nights. Unfortunately I developed a bit of a throat infection, but I hoped nobody would notice.

The video of the concert is fun and summery – the set had bright lights and palm trees and the singers were dressed almost as we did in *Summer Holiday*, in white T-shirts and tight pants. We wanted to create the atmosphere of a summer party, with lots of pop, and I was very happy with the upbeat result – even the weather was kind.

The closing number called for a rather more serious song. Our dear friend John Seymour, who had played a major part in stage design for our concerts over the last twenty years, died the week before we played Hyde Park. He is sadly missed. He was well known to my fans too, and his work was much appreciated by them. So I felt the audience understood when I said a public goodbye to John on stage and ended on the Sunday night with *It's In Every One Of Us*, a song which featured in *Time*. It felt very appropriate to revive it as a tribute to John.

I may have officially started my sabbatical year this summer of 1999 but as I write, sitting under the vast blue Portuguese skies, I am really already looking forward to the millennium concerts in Birmingham.

Millennium celebrations in London seem to be very much centred on the Dome and as far as I am aware there are no big live concerts being played in the capital. In Birmingham, however, the city's celebration programme is centred on the National Indoor Arena. I am delighted to be playing in Birmingham for this historic occasion – after London, Birmingham is the city in which I've performed most, in fact I've played at the NIA and the NEC more than any other artist. It was in Birmingham that fans queued on a winter's night for the opening of *Heathcliff*. I also remember very fondly – and I hope a few Brummies do, too – the fourteen back-to-back concerts I played at the NEC in 1990 and again in 1992.

To welcome the new millennium, Birmingham City Council has planned a series of spectacular entertainment, arts and cultural events. I know it will be the thrill of a lifetime to be part of the celebrations. There are to be nine 'Countdown' concerts in the last two weeks of 1999 and then a concert on Millennium Eve, which will be beamed on to big

screens in Birmingham's Central Square. I've
thought a lot about how I can put something extra
into the concerts in order to add a little excitement
to the occasion. I also wanted to donate something
that represented a part of the passing century, and
I've come upon the idea of donating my 1959 Ford
Thunderbird convertible.

All the concert tickets carry numbers and
the owner of the ticket number drawn at the
Millennium Eve concert will win my all-time
favourite dream machine. It has a red interior,
5700cc V8 petrol engine, and in November, in the
run up to the concerts, it is to be displayed at the
International Classic Motor Show at the National
Exhibition Centre.

The charity we've chosen to benefit from all
proceeds from the Millennium Eve Concert is
Children's Promise. It is an affiliation of seven major
children's charities, and is asking people all over the
UK to donate their final hour's earnings of this
millennium to benefit the children of the next.
When I think of the future I think of children and of
how different childhood is now from when I grew
up. And yet there are still many deprived and
suffering children in need of help in our
technological society. If we can communicate one
hope for the Internet generation it must be a
willingness to help young lives under threat.

I think the majority of people associate the
start of the twenty-first century with renewal and
would wish to see the new era celebrated by
'putting something back into the community'.
Prime Minister Tony Blair has publicly endorsed the
Children's Promise project, so we're expecting at
least an hour's salary from him!

The Millennium Eve concert is also a very
positive thing to look forward to while I've been
sitting on the beach this summer – the booking
office in Birmingham has sold thousands of tickets

Cliff Richard

Behind the wheel of my wonderful 1959
Ford Thunderbird

I also wanted to donate something that represented a part of the passing century, and I've come upon the idea of donating my 1959 Ford Thunderbird convertible. All the concert tickets carry numbers and the owner of the ticket number drawn at the Millennium Eve concert will win my all-time favourite dream machine. It has a red interior, 5700cc V8 petrol engine, and in November, in the run up to the concerts, it is to be displayed at the International Classic Motor Show at the National Exhibition Centre.

Cliff

Having performed with Hank Marvin in the past I knew he was the artist that I needed to help get the party atmosphere going for my Millennium Eve charity concert in Birmingham,

already and predicts that the concerts may be a sell out! I am so grateful for the opportunity to make a very public and practical commitment to the future by contributing to Children's Promise.

The first person I thought of to join me on stage was Hank Marvin. 'I know it's New Year's Eve and everything, Hank, but do you think you could spare a few hours to do Birmingham with me?' I asked him.

Hank hesitated for a full millisecond before replying, 'Yes!'

With Hank on board I know we're already guaranteed a great party on stage – and I'm hoping that other musicians will join me on Millennium Eve. Just before the concert starts I will light a flame of hope, which represents Jesus the Light of the World. My great desire is for the world to have an accelerated spiritual awakening, and I know many of you share that hope.

I do know that 00:00 hours on 1 January 2000 will be a wonderful moment for me and many others, because my audiences will have created a brand new source of hope for Children's Promise.

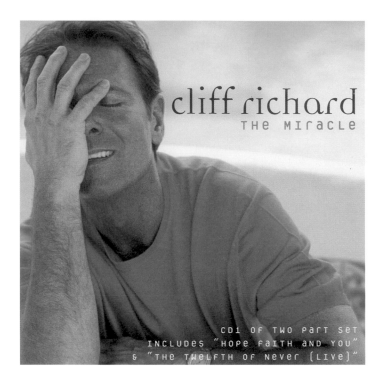

The Miracle, a track from my Real As I Wanna Be album, was recorded live at the memorable Albert Hall concerts in March 1999.

I've decided that for me the year 2000 is the time to take a sabbatical – at least that's what you would call it in any other profession. But when I announced my plan to take a year off there were immediately rumours of my retirement owing to fatigue, emotional crisis and other wacky theories. I hope I've made it very clear that no, I'm *not* retiring – I've no intention of stopping singing voluntarily. Two good reasons to choose the year 2000 as a break are the millennium and my sixtieth birthday on the horizon.

Apart from a concert I've promised to do in the West Country for Jill Dando's favourite charity and a Christian festival in Glastonbury, I just want to keep a clean slate and experience an empty diary after so many years of a relentlessly schedule-driven life.

Just to have days on end to spend with my family and friends, in any month other than August, will be a revolutionary change in my life. I'm not going to spend an age remodelling my home or doing anything domestic; it's more or less as I want it since I had a conservatory built last year, having done hardly anything to the house since I first bought it. I'm an uncle twenty times over so I've hordes of nephews and nieces and I'll be able to spend more time with them next year.

I like to think of myself as a person who can adjust my thinking to whatever I'm doing at the time and give that project 100 per cent focus. I'm like that on stage, at rehearsals, at a party – even when I'm playing tennis (which I know I've no hope of excelling at), I still give it my best. Now I am absolutely confident that I can be very disciplined about focusing on nothing else but leisure for a while!

Top of my leisure wish-list of plane tickets is a trip Down Under. I've always tremendously enjoyed working in Australia, but in all these years I have never had time to enjoy it as a tourist, so I'm stocking up on the guide books and topping up the sun cream.

I know there have been rumours about my working on a musical of my own life and while it's true that since *Heathcliff* I've longed to work on another musical, I could certainly think of subjects that would be more challenging than myself! No, musicals are definitely not on the cards for 2000 because I'm going to switch right out of work and right into relaxation. There's a time for everything and this is my time to become a global tourist. See you in 2001.

Sometimes I feel that the
audience almost likes me
more than they like my
music. I'm not saying that
is a fact, but it feels like
that to me — it feels as
though even if
I had no band and just
went out there and talked
to them we'd
still have a good time.

Cliff Richard   * 211

A Celebration

Singles

Stronger Than That/Joanna

Silhouettes/The Winner

From A DIstance/Lindsay Jane

Saviour's Day/The Oh Boy Melody

More To Life/Mo's Theme

We Should Be Together/ Miss You Nights,

This New Year/Scarlet Ribbons

I Still Believe In You/Bulange Downpour

Peace In Our TIme/Somebody Loves You

Human Work Of Art/Ragged

Never Let Go/Congratulations

Healing Love/Yesterday's Memories/Carrie,

All I Have To Do Is Dream

(with Phil Everly)/Miss You Nights

Misunderstood Man/Misunderstood Man

(instrumental) October

Can't Keep This Feeling In

Albums

From A Distance – The Event

Together With Cliff Richard

My Kinda Life (French import)

Cliff Richard – The Album

Songs From Heathcliff

Real As I Wanna Be

Photographic Credits

Every effort has been made to contact and acknowledge correctly the source and copyright holder of the illustrations in this book, and André Deutsch apologises for any unintentional errors or omissions, which will be corrected in future editions.

The publishers would like to thank the Cliff Richard Organisation and EMI
for all their help with the illustrative content of this book.

Ronald Grant Archive: 1, 12 (top), 26, 30-31, 32, 33, 34 (2), 35, 37, 55, 56, 64-5, 66 (2), 68-9, 72, 77, 80, 81 (right), 85, 154-5

Paul Cox: 125, 126, 139, 147 (2), 156, 160, 161 (2), 164-5, 175, 178 (right), 179, 184, 186, 206

Paul Cox/Chester Hopkins International: 159, 170, 171, 172, 173

Paul Cox/EMI: 6, 187, 193 (left), 204, 207, 210-11, 212, 214-5

David Steen: 19, 48

Associated Press: 21, 145

Daily Sketch: 23, 42, 51, 76-7, 78-9

Sport & General: 47

Daily Herald: 63

Western Mail: 113

London Features International: 114-15, 119, 191, 202

Doug McKenzie: 120-21

Harry de Louw: 123

Mirror Syndication International: 128, 129, 131, 183 (left), 196, 198-9, 200, 208, 209

Gered Mankowitz: 130

EMI/Simon Fowler: 150

Rex Features: 151

Redferns: 91, 162, 167, 182

All Action: 140-41, 163, 166, 168, 174, 176-7 (2), 183 (right), 185 (2), 188-90, 193 (right), 201, 203, 205, 213

Popperfoto: 180-81

PA News: 192, 197

Joan Batten: 100